Modern Hotel and Motel Management

Second Edition

Modern Hotel and Motel Management

Gerald W. Lattin

School of Hotel Administration,
Cornell University

 W. H. Freeman and Company

San Francisco

PRINTED IN THE UNITED STATES OF AMERICA

LIBRARY OF CONGRESS CATALOG CARD NUMBER: 68-21282
STANDARD BOOK NUMBER 7167 0914-7

2 3 4 5 6 7 8 9

Preface to the Second Edition

As the Preface to the first edition stated, MODERN HOTEL MANAGEMENT was designed to provide in one book the satisfaction of several needs: an introduction to the field of hotel management, an explanation of the complex interrelationships involved in this business, and an insight into the variety of vocational opportunities available. The first edition was well received and has been employed as a text or a reference in all the United States colleges offering training in hotel management.

The hotel industry has developed and changed considerably in the ten years the book has been in print. This revision reflects these changes. Undoubtedly the greatest change has occurred in the motel or motor hotel field, the discussion of which I have attempted to bring completely up to date—the new title of the book reflects this emphasis. Tourism has become the world's largest industry and in this edition receives the attention it merits. The discussion of the Personnel Department has been expanded and the treatment of other departments brought up to date.

Chapter 8, A Look At The Future, is completely new. Crystal-ball gazing is both hazardous and fascinating. In writing this chapter, I called freely on the thoughts and ideas of numerous members of the faculty of the School of Hotel Administration at Cornell University. Special thanks go to Mr. Leslie Bond and Mr. H. Alexander MacLennan for their contributions to the topics of food service and data processing.

I am indebted to many friends in the hotel industry who willingly gave of their time and knowledge and to many of my colleagues in the educational world who have sent along suggestions and ideas. A very special vote of thanks goes to my wife for her encouragement and gentle persuasion.

It is my hope that this book will prove a useful tool to educational and vocational counselors, hotel training directors, and teachers of hotel management.

Ithaca, New York GERALD W. LATTIN
January 1968

Preface to the First Edition

MODERN HOTEL MANAGEMENT was designed to fill several areas of need which have become increasingly apparent to me during my eleven years' association with the hotel industry. The book is a direct result of my experience in introducing the students of the School of Hotel Administration at Cornell University to the numerous facets of the hotel industry.

The varied nature of hotel work and the many occupational opportunities it affords seem to me to have been but vaguely understood by the very audience the industry should attract: the general working population, and young high school graduates. *Modern Hotel Management* should provide much of the information required to enlighten this segment of the population. Hotels and hotel associations will find the book a useful means for disseminating information about their industry, as well as a recruitment aid. Educational and vocational counselors will find it a beneficial addition to their libraries of vocational information.

With hotels attaching increased importance to induction programs designed to familiarize employees with all phases of their particular operation, a book such as this should prove a usable training tool.

I am indebted to many friends in the hotel industry who willingly gave of their time and knowledge, both of which were invaluable aids in the preparation of this book. Mr. Edward J. Smith of the Sheraton Corporation of America contributed the chapter on the catering department. Mr. Charles O'Toole and Mr. Karl Mehlmann of Denver's Brown Palace Hotel were extremely helpful in providing illustrative as well as textual material. Special thanks go to Mr. Wallace Lee and Mr. Ruel Tyo for their contributions to the chapter on opportunities. Without their help this book could not have been written.

Ithaca, New York   GERALD W. LATTIN
May, 1958

Contents

Part One

An Introduction to
Hotel Management

CHAPTER 1

Growth and Development
of the Hotel Industry

EARLY INNS

A history of the hotel industry, to be absolutely complete, would necessarily go back some twelve thousand years; however, from a practical standpoint innkeeping as such was not possible until the adoption of a standardized medium of exchange. With the establishment of money at some time in the sixth century B.C. came the first real impetus for people to trade and travel. Then, as the traveler's radius of movement widened, his need for lodging became greater. Early inns were nothing more than small parts of private dwellings. Typically, the inns were self-service institutions, rarely clean, and more often than not they were run by disreputable and unprogressive landlords. These conditions prevailed with little, if any, change for several hundreds of years.

Not until the Industrial Revolution occurred in England were there signs of progress and new ideas in the business of innkeeping. During the era from 1750 to 1820 English inns gained the reputation of being the finest in the world; their early development was centered in and around London where innkeepers increased services, maintained standards of cleanliness, and, to some extent, catered to the guests. As highways were improved, the new ideas that originated in the metropolitan area were adopted by the countryside inns. The inns of England reached their peak of development during the Pickwickian period; then, for some reason, the English innkeeper fell into a rut and became either unwilling or unable to institute further progress.

In the colonies, early inns were located at the seaport towns and were patterned directly after those of the mother country. But while the English landlord was content to remain in a status quo of restrictive apathy, his American counterpart demonstrated no such inhibitions. The American innkeeper was a radical, a gambler, and an expansionist. Shortly after the Revolution, American inns were the largest in the world and were well on their way to offering the finest services available anywhere. Admittedly, in terms of present-day standards these services would be totally inadequate, but for their time they were optimum. By 1800 it was evident that the United States was assuming leadership in the development of the modern first-class hotel. Besides the pioneering spirit of the American innkeeper, several other factors influenced the rapid rise of the hotel industry in the United States. While European hotels operated on the premise that only the aristocracy was entitled to luxury and comfort, American hotels were run for equalitarian enjoyment—anyone could take advantage of the services of a hotel as long as he could pay for them, and the rates were within the means of almost everyone. Another factor was the American habit of living permanently in hotels. Another, and probably the most important factor, was the fact that the average American did considerably more traveling than did the residents of other countries. In fact, this extensive traveling habit of Americans has continued to be a tremendous influence, even to the present day, on the entire hotel industry at home and abroad.

THE AMERICAN HOTEL

1794-1829

It was in 1794 when the City Hotel—the first building erected specifically for hotel purposes in America—opened in New York City. Until this time innkeepers had merely converted their own or someone else's home into an inn. The City Hotel was actually an overgrown inn, but with its seventy-three rooms it was considered by everyone to be an "immense establishment." It quickly became the social center of New York which at that time was a booming town of 30,000 population. Boston, Baltimore, and Philadelphia, not to be outdone by New York City, quickly opened similar establishments. In Boston it was the Exchange Coffee House, in Baltimore the City Hotel, and in Philadelphia the Mansion House, that became fashionable meeting places. (It is interesting to note that New York's first skyscraper was the Adelphi Hotel—a building of six-story construction). The era of the overgrown inn spanned a thirty-five year period and set the stage for the first golden age of hotels in the United States.

1829-1900

In 1829 the first-class hotel was born in Boston. The Tremont House richly deserves the title "The Adam and Eve of the Modern Hotel Industry"—it was conceded to be something absolutely new in hotelkeeping, and it surpassed its contemporaries both in America and in Europe. The Tremont was the largest and costliest building that had ever been erected in this country. The architect, Isaiah Rogers, became the leading authority on hotel construction, and he strongly influenced hotel architecture for the next fifty years. It is generally acknowledged, although the Swiss may disagree, that the opening of the Tremont established America's supremacy in the science of hotel management.

In addition to its size, cost, and extreme luxuriousness, the Tremont had many innovations which made it a favorite topic of conversation among all who had been there. The typical inn of the day consisted of one or two large rooms containing from three to ten beds. The beds were large and could accommodate several people at one time, and an innkeeper never considered it a profitable night unless each bed was occupied by a minimum of two guests. The Tremont was the first hotel to feature private single and double rooms; for those who valued privacy, this must have seemed like a dream come true. Not only were there private rooms, but each door had a lock! Two other new ideas were considered the extreme of luxury: every room was equipped with a bowl and a pitcher, and every room was supplied with free soap. Under the management of the Boyden family, a complete staff was hired, trained, and instructed that a guest should be treated with dignity and respect. French cuisine was introduced, for the first time in a hotel; the Tremont had the first bellboys; and the annunciator—the forerunner of the room telephone—was introduced there.

The Tremont initiated up-to-date hotel development but soon fell victim to the trend it had started. Other cities took up the challenge of building finer hotels, and within twenty years the Tremont had to close for modernizing. Its life span was exactly sixty-five years, but during the last twenty it was a second-class hotel.

Throughout most of the nineteenth century the contest among hotelmen to build better, larger, and more luxurious hotels continued. Every city in the nation wanted a hotel as good as the Tremont had been, in spite of the fact that often there was insufficient business to warrant such an operation. The theory seemed to be that no city amounted to much which did not have at least one hotel to impress visitors with the greatness and hospitality of the community.

Even with the westward movement of more and more people, the hotel boom was not left behind. The excitement and competition of hotel building which was at its peak between 1830 and 1850 in the East went on and on all the way to the Pacific Coast. Chicago had the Grand Pacific, the Palmer House, and the Sherman House; St. Louis pointed with pride to the Planters; and Omaha extolled the virtues of the Paxton. San Francisco built the Palace—the most ornate and expensive hotel of its day. The Palace never made money, but in appearance, structure, equipment, and lavishness it was a real triumph.

Near the end of the nineteenth century the hotel boom quieted, and most people were of the opinion that every possible convenience, service, and new idea had been incorporated in the country's modern hotels. Little did they realize that within a few years the world's greatest hotelman would be building a hotel so new that it would be called an invention and that it would set the standards for twentieth century hotel construction and management.

The intense competition between cities and between hotelmen to build the biggest and best hotel resulted in considerable deviation from the American tradition of hotels designed for equalitarian enjoyment. At the close of the nineteenth century there were many elegant, luxurious establishments, typified by New York's old Waldorf-Astoria, Denver's Brown Palace, and San Francisco's Palace. At the other extreme were the small hotels built close to railroad stations; these were little more than overgrown rooming houses, and because of their inadequacies they were often not too desirable a place for a traveler to make his headquarters. Many a person of modest means found the luxury hotels too expensive and the small hotels lacking in standards of service, meals, and cleanliness. As a result, he was forced to choose one of two evils, and whatever his choice was, he was seldom content.

At the turn of the century there were two new developments in the United States that were to influence twentieth century hotel operation. First, as the country's economy expanded, the commercial traveler became increasingly prominent in the business world. As this group grew in number, there developed a corresponding increasing need for suitable hotel accommodations and conveniences to serve it. Second, improvements in transportation made travel easier and less expensive. In a society seemingly ever restless and eager to be on the move, such a development immediately led to a tremendous upsurge in the number of travelers. Once travel expenses came within the means of the middle class of American society, it became an entirely new segment of the traveling public.

1900-1930

At the very beginning of the twentieth century the hotel industry was confronted with the challenge of serving a new traveling population. It had to face such problems as: What type of accommodations were needed by the traveling salesman? Were new services necessary? Would these accommodations and services appeal to the middle-class traveler, or was an entirely different type of operation necessary to meet his demands? What rates would attract business and still provide a fair profit? Answers to these questions were not immediately available. Fortunately, for the industry, Ellsworth M. Statler had foreseen the development of just such a situation and was ready to meet the challenge himself; while leaders in the field were arguing the pros and cons of various suggestions, he was drawing plans for his first hotel. By 1907 construction was under way in Buffalo on the Statler Hotel.

The opening of the Buffalo Statler on January 18, 1908,

marked a new age in the American hotel industry—this was the birth of the modern commercial hotel. In this "invention" (for as truly as Henry Ford invented the modern automobile, Ellsworth Statler invented the modern hotel) were embodied all the known techniques of the day, plus a lifetime of Statler's own experiences and ideas which he had carefully recorded in notebooks. Many services and conveniences that are taken for granted today, but which were innovations then, were first introduced in this hotel: fire doors protecting the two main stairways, a door lock with the keyhole above the knob so that it could be easily located in a dark hall, a light switch just inside the door to eliminate groping through the room in the dark, a private bath, a full-length mirror, and circulating ice water for every room, a free morning newspaper for each guest. With such accommodations, no wonder the slogan of the Statler was, "A Room and a Bath for a Dollar and a Half." Besides those singularities designed to increase guest comfort, the hotel contained many new structural and engineering designs, and because of them the Statler became the model for modern hotel construction for the next forty years. Truly here was a modern hotel that provided comfort, service, and cleanliness for the average man at a price within his budget. Immediate public response assured the success of the Statler Hotel and initiated the development of the Statler Hotel Company.

Following the excitement engendered by the first Statler Hotel there was a time of relative inactivity in the development of the hotel industry This was enforced in part by World War I. But the period from 1910 to 1920 turned out to be only the quiet before the storm, for the prosperous Roaring Twenties ushered in the second golden age of hotels. It was then that hotel construction reached an all-time peak, both in numbers built and dollars expended. Just as businessmen thought there was no limit to the nation's prosperity, so did hotelmen consider limitless the demand for hotel services and space, and during this brief period were built many of today's most famous hotels. New York's Hotel

Pennsylvania (now the Statler) was the world's largest when it opened. It was only a matter of a few years until Ralph Hitz's Hotel New Yorker surpassed the Pennsylvania as New York's largest hotel. But in 1927 the giant of them all—the Stevens Hotel —opened in Chicago. With its 3,000 rooms the Stevens (recently renamed the Conrad Hilton) took over the title "The World's Largest Hotel," and to this day it maintains that distinction. It seems doubtful that a larger hotel will ever be built, but one look at the past clearly shows how unpredictable the hotel business can be. Two luxury hotels which were started during this era were the present Waldorf-Astoria and the Pierre, both in New York. Large cities and name hotels had no monopoly on the building fever of the twenties—cities and towns everywhere were acquiring new hotels. Some were financed by the communities, some by corporations, and some by private individuals, but the enthusiasm was shared by all.

The Depression

Then, just as bigger and better plans were being readied, the bubble burst and hotels dropped from a golden age into the unhappiest period of hotel history. In 1930 when the country plunged into the Great Depression, hotel rooms were emptied and business sank to an all-time low. So severe were the effects of the depression that 85 percent of the nation's hotels went either into receivership or through some form of liquidation. Many financial experts openly expressed the opinion that the hotel industry would never recover. Even later, when the economy in general showed definite signs of recovery, investors considered hotels to be white elephants (the supply of hotel rooms seemed too great for any future demand) and were unwilling to put their dollars into them. Here, credit must be given to the hotel operators. Many lost their savings and their business, but the majority of them never lost faith and remained to guide the industry through its darkest hour.

World War II

By 1940 the industry was slowly stabilizing at a level which, although considerably below that of the twenties, brought mild optimism about the future to a few hotelmen. However, not even the most optimistic envisioned the tremendous upswing that was to occur only two years later. The outbreak of World War II set into motion the greatest mass movement this country has ever experienced. Millions of Americans went into the armed services, millions more moved to concentrated areas of defense plants, thousands of others—those coordinating the defense program— found it necessary to travel. With this activity in full force, the demand for hotel rooms and services reached an all-time peak, and it became a common sight to see people sleeping in lobbies because there just weren't enough rooms available. The hotel world had never experienced nor expected such a situation. Undoubtedly, the war years presented the greatest single challenge ever faced by the industry. The individual operator had capacity business every day in the week in spite of the fact that often he had lost half of his complement of trained professional staff to the armed services. Because most hotels were understaffed, they were forced to employ large numbers of people who had absolutely no hotel experience. Standards of service necessarily suffered, but the fact that service was even maintained is amazing, considering the handicaps under which hotels had to operate. Although they were never classified as an essential industry, hotels can feel justly proud of their contribution to the nation's war effort.

Fifties

The prosperity of the war years continued through 1947, with hotels running above 90 percent occupancy. In 1948 a downward trend of business was noticeable and more or less set the scene for the 1950's. A quick glance at the graphs on the following page

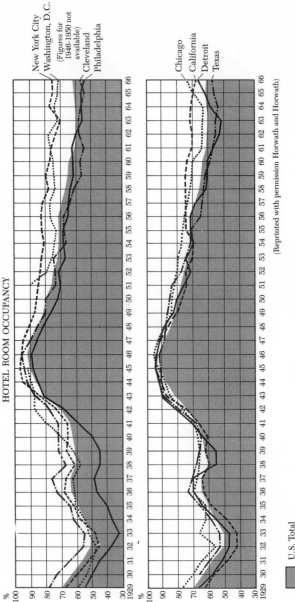

HOTEL ROOM OCCUPANCY

New York City
Washington, D.C.
(Figures for 1946-1950 not available)
Cleveland
Philadelphia

Chicago
California
Detroit
Texas

U. S. Total

(Reprinted with permission Horwath and Horwath)

shows the general downward trend in hotel occupancy during this ten-year period.

Unlike the Twenties, the Fifties did not give rise to a boom in the building of major hotels. A few were built, but the major area of growth was in motels and in motor hotels. The Los Angeles Statler Hilton, which opened on October 27, 1952, was thought to be a trend setter in hotel construction. One complete wing of the building is devoted to leasable office space, the theory being that rental income from the offices would serve to stabilize the hotel's financial structure by carrying fixed costs of operation during the slack periods of the year. No one, to my knowledge, has disputed the validity of the theory, but few, if any, of the later hotels have followed the pattern.

Although noted as a period of many new developments, the 1950's will go down in history as the period when the motel and the motor hotel really came of age. In retrospect it is easy to explain the phenomenal growth and success of this segment of the hospitality industry. More and more, the American family was traveling as a unit and the mode of transportation was the automobile. The habits, tastes, and desires of the motoring public had undergone a considerable change. A new note of informality had come into the American way of life. Suddenly there was a way to eliminate formal dress, lobby parades, tipping, and parking problems—by going to the motel. The rooms were new with modern furniture, wall-to-wall carpeting, and television, a swimming pool was often an added attraction, and then there was the convenience of your own transportation.

At first, many hotelmen had difficulty deciding just what role the motel would play in the industry. To many it was a "flash in the pan" or a novelty that would soon wear out and fade away. To others it was a new kind of competition and it had to be licked. The more farsighted hotelmen recognized that motels represented progress and quickly adopted the theory "if you can't lick them, join them." Slowly but surely, established hotel companies moved into the motel business.

Unfortunately for the industry, much of the time between 1950 and 1960 was spent in endless arguments on the general topic of hotel versus motel. At times, an observer might well have believed that the two were arch enemies whose interests were completely incompatible. Slowly the truth of the whole situation became more obvious—motels and motor hotels were not a new and different industry at all. They were very much an integral part of the hospitality industry. What they represented was a new concept in the art of innkeeping. Some very alert individuals had recognized a need of the American public and had produced a product that would fulfill this need. As more and more hotel and motel people recognized this fact, suspicion and enmity turned to cooperation and understanding. A significant milestone was erected when the American Hotel Association changed its name to the American Hotel and Motel Association. Not all the problems have been resolved, but the atmsophere is improving daily.

Once the motel boom got underway, it took off like a rocket. When one looks at the industry today, it is hard to believe that the origin was in the little roadside cabins and motels that were occasional dots on the landscape. As shown in Table 1, from 1939 to 1962 there were 36,000 new motels built in the United States. Although the early motels were small and generally operated by a man and wife team, a change took place in the 1950's. Motels were growing in size (number of units) and in plushness and service. With increased size came additional burdens of management, which many times eliminated the "mom and pop" style of operation. Professional management became not only desirable, but often mandatory.

In the early 1950's a 50-room motel was a real giant. Within a few years, however, it wasn't even average size. That is how rapidly the increase in size occurred. Practically all new motels built in the late fifties and early sixties contained a minimum of 80 rooms and averaged close to 100. In fact, the size explosion created a problem of terminology or classification. Soon the large

TABLE 1   Growth Pattern of Hotels and Motels
in Number and Total Receipts

Year	Hotels		Motels	
1939	Number	29,000	Number	14,000
	Receipts	$ 875,000,000	Receipts	$ 37,000,000
1962	Number	29,000	Number	50,000
	Receipts	$3,000,000,000	Receipts	$1,500,000,000
1965	Number	28,107	Number	61,550
	Receipts	$4,000,000,000	Receipts	$6,100,000,000

motels were being called motor hotels and thus came the difficulty of differentiating between a motel and a hotel or between either of them and a motor hotel.

Initially it was said that a motel was constructed horizontally and a hotel vertically, plus the fact that the hotel offered a much more complete roster of services. Soon the motels became multistoried, and then the larger motels instituted all the usual hotel services. A new definition had to be sought. In reality, the only difference between the traditional hotel and a motel or motor hotel is that parking is always available at motels and motor hotels. Perhaps the safest phrase is "motels are becoming more and more like hotels, while hotels are becoming more and more like motels." A fine example of this trend is the San Francisco Hilton. The inner core of the building is a parking garage around which are built the guest rooms. The guest arriving by automobile drives into the motor entrance, registers from his car seat at the motor desk and then drives his car to the floor where his room is located. Having parked his car, he steps through a door into the hotel corridor, finds his room and settles down for a pleasant stay. He has reached his room with no lobby parade, no formality, no tipping, his car is practically outside his door, and every service is as close as the phone in his room. One might well ask, "Is the San Francisco Hilton a motel, a hotel, or a motor

TABLE 2   Motor Hotels in the United States
Size and Number, by State, December 1, 1965

Rank By Number of Units	Motor Hotels	State	Number of Units	Number of Motor Hotels	Average Number of Units Per Motor Hotel
1	1	California	54,438	546	100
2	2	Florida	44,785	469	95
3	3	Texas	35,766	355	101
4	4	New York	26,607	240	111
5	7	Illinois	20,816	172	121
6	5	Ohio	20,255	199	102
7	8	Pennsylvania	18,287	159	115
8	6	New Jersey	15,704	174	90
9	11	Georgia	13,744	127	108
10	9	Virginia	13,574	144	94
11	12	Arizona	12,399	123	101
12	15	Missouri	12,378	104	110
13	10	North Carolina	10,946	134	82
14	13	Massachusetts	10,742	117	92
15	14	Michigan	10,247	117	88
16	16	Alabama	9,291	93	100
17	19	Louisiana	9,096	81	112
18	18	Indiana	8,533	87	98
19	17	Tennessee	8,509	89	96
20	20	Maryland	7,275	73	100
21	23	Kentucky	6,938	69	101
22	22	Wisconsin	6,910	71	97
23	21	Oklahoma	6,568	72	91
24	26	Arkansas	6,478	63	103
25	24	Nevada	6,344	68	93
26	25	Colorado	6,204	68	91
27	27	Mississippi	5.638	63	89
28	28	Washington	5,625	61	92
29	31	Minnesota	5,571	57	98
30	32	Iowa	5,335	52	103
31	30	New Mexico	5,221	58	90
32	29	South Carolina	4,943	61	81
33	33	Connecticut	4,933	52	95
34	34	Kansas	4,792	52	92

TABLE 2, *Continued*   Motor Hotels in the United States
Size and Number, by State, December 1, 1965

Rank By Number of Units	Rank By Number of Motor Hotels	State	Number of Units	Number of Motor Hotels	Average Number of Units Per Motor Hotel
35	35	Oregon	4,679	52	90
36	36	Utah	3,978	35	114
37	40	District of Columbia	3,631	19	191
38	37	Nebraska	3,118	31	101
39	39	Maine	2,371	27	88
40	38	Wyoming	2,353	29	81
41	41	Delaware	1,598	19	84
42	42	Idaho	1,583	19	83
43	43	South Dakota	1,580	19	83
44	45	New Hampshire	1,571	17	92
45	46	West Virginia	1,528	15	102
46	44	Montana	1,387	18	77
47	47	North Dakota	1,190	12	99
48	48	Vermont	859	12	72
49	49	Rhode Island	614	6	102
		Total United States	476,932	4,800	99

hotel?" It is called a hotel by the owners. For statistical purposes today, people in the industry denote properties with 40 rooms or fewer as motels and those with more than 40 rooms as motor hotels. Stephen W. Brener, well-known real estate and motel expert, defines a motor hotel as "a property with transient lodging facilities, built or completely modernized since World War II, open all year, and containing at least 50 guest units, plus adequate on-premises free parking."

Motels and motor hotels, in their brief history, have similarities with the older hotels. Both groups were originally composed primarily of independent operators. It was inevitable, however—with the growth in size, increase in complexity, and absentee ownership—that chain operation would enter the field. Within a very few years, chain operation has made heavy inroads into the motel field. According to available statistics, 28.4 percent of the hotels in the United States are now chain operated, and 36 percent of the motels and motor hotels belong to chains. As impressive as these figures are, they fail to give a complete picture. Because the chains tend to own and operate the larger properties, nearly 50 percent of the total hotel rooms and 60 percent of the motel rooms in the country earn daily revenue for chain management.

It is interesting to follow the distribution and development of motor hotels both geographically and within a given metropolitan area. The first and most rapid development of motor hotels occurred in California and in the western area of the United States. The second area to expand was the South, particularly Florida and Texas. Through the 1950's and the early 1960's a definite geographical shift is quite evident. California still leads in both number of motor hotels and number of units, but today most motor hotels are in the East. Table 2 illustrates the geographical distribution of motor hotels in the United States as compiled by Mr. Stephen Brener. California even today, for example, has more motor hotels than the Midwest and New England combined.

Within any given area, the motor hotels first grew up along the highway outside the city and slowly formed a ring around the city. The outskirts were considered to be the ideal location, and very few of the experts believed that we would ever see a motor hotel in the center of town or even in the town anywhere. As if to emphasize the rapid change nature of the hospitality industry, motor hotels began to appear within many downtown areas. The success of these downtown locations is attested to by the continued growth of city motor hotels. Because of the high cost of land in the city, these motor hotels must be of the high-rise variety. Being the most recently built, they are also larger, following the general size trend of the new motor hotels. In New York City, for example, the City Squire Motor Hotel as 727 rooms and the Holiday Inn has 600 rooms. Table 3 shows the leading cities in the motor hotel industry.

Earlier in this chapter we noted the decline in hotel occupancy rates throughout the 1950's. This decline occurred in spite of a rapidly increasing amount of travel and number of people needing away-from-home accommodations. Obviously these peo-

TABLE 3   Leading Cities in the United States Motor Hotel Industry (Over 3,000 Rental Units) as of December 1, 1965

City°	Number of Units	Percent of Total Units in State	Number of Motor Hotels	Average Number of Units Per Motor Hotel in City	in State
Miami Beach, Fla.	9,345	20.9%	80	117	95
New York City, N.Y.	6,915	26.0%	37	187	111
Chicago, Ill.	6,806	32.7%	41	166	121
Atlantic City, N.J.	5,272	33.6%	44	120	90
Atlanta, Ga.	4,978	36.2%	33	151	108
Dallas, Tex.	4,814	13.5%	36	134	101
Houston, Tex.	4,714	13.2%	38	124	101
Phoenix, Ariz.	4,642	37.4%	43	108	101
Las Vegas, Nev.	4,453	70.2%	46	97	93
Los Angeles, Calif.	4,173	7.7%	32	130	100
Fort Lauderdale, Fla.	3,835	8.6%	32	120	95
St. Louis, Mo.	3,758	30.4%	25	150	110
Cleveland, Ohio	3,692	18.2%	28	132	102
Washington, D.C.	3,631	100.0%	19	191	191
New Orleans, La.	3,361	37.0%	24	140	112
San Francisco, Calif.	3,190	5.9%	23	139	100
Columbus, Ohio	3,029	15.0%	22	138	102
Total 17 Cities	80,608	16.9%°°	603	134	99°°°

°Does not include suburbs.

°°17 cities as percent of U.S. total.

°°°Average number of units for U.S. as a whole.

ple found rooms and where they found them, of course, was in the motels and motor hotels. Here then is the principal reason for the hotelman's concern about the mushrooming motel industry. Rooms business is by far the most profitable aspect of hotel management and hotels suddenly found this profitable business disappearing at a rapid rate. The hotels in the smaller cities were the first to receive the full brunt of the motel competition and the attrition rate shot up alarmingly. Within a few years many of these hotels disappeared and were replaced by parking lots; others were converted to non-hotel usage and some were simply closed.

A case study of City Y will illustrate what was happening all over the country. In 1946, City Y's hotels had a combined total of 3,970 rooms and the occupancy rate for the year was 87 percent. Total sales for the year were $1,260,710. In 1960, City Y hotels had 3,730 hotel rooms with an occupancy rate of 63 percent. However, City Y now had 3,920 motel rooms with a 69 percent occupancy. The hotels had total sales of $857,750, and the motels sales were $987,325. More people were staying overnight and spending more money, but the hotels were losing both patronage and profits to the newer motels and motor hotels.

What does the future hold for the motel division of the hospitality industry? No one can be sure when predicting the future, but most experts agree that the great building period is probably over. Undoubtedly in three or four years there will be a decrease in the number of motels in this country. At the same time there will be an increase in the number of rental units available. The annual report of *The Tourist Court Journal* for 1966 (Table 4) predicts that the current 2,400,000 units will grow to 3,000,000 by 1970. The current 61,550 motels will diminish to 58,400 in the same period. The motels going out of business will be the smaller ones, and those to be constructed will be larger than the current average. The prediction then is for more rental units concentrated in fewer but larger motels.

A final note on motel development must re-emphasize the

TABLE 4   Motel Fact Sheet—1966

Motel Sizes by Number of Rental Units	Total Number of Motels by Size	Percent of Total Motels by Size	Total Number of Rental Units	Percent of Total Rental Units	Number of Motels with Food Facility	Percent of Motels with Food Facility
10 and Under	7,936	12.9%	63,488	3.1%	151	1.9%
11–20	21,409	34.8%	363,953	17.9%	2,119	9.9%
21–40	18,210	29.6%	564,510	27.8%	7,502	41.2%
41–60	7,445	12.1%	409,475	20.2%	6,522	87.6%
61–100	4,923	8.0%	418,455	20.6%	4,756	96.6%
101 and Over	1,627	2.6%	210,279	10.4%	1,589	99.5%
Total	61,550	100.0%	2,030,160	100.0%	22,639	36.8%

Invested Capital $18,285,397,100
Gross Annual Sales and Income . . . . . . $ 6,133,149,750
Persons Accommodated During 1965 . . .   975,567,255

Reprinted with Permission: Tourist Court Journal, Temple, Texas

fantastic growth of the motel industry in the 1950's. Of today's motels, .9 percent were built before 1930, 3.6 percent in the thirties, 16.3 percent in the forties, 50.7 percent in the fifties, and 23.5 percent since 1960.

Referral Organizations and Franchise Developments

Two other developments which received great impetus during the 1950's were Referral Associations and the Franchise movement, particularly with regard to motels and motor hotels. As the motel chains grew, the independent operator found himself in a tough competitive position. American travelers generally have reacted to a "brand name" or "brand identification symbol." The chains, of course, had a ready-made brand name or symbol which they promoted with great success. A chain motel was easily recognized by the facilities, the rather standardized architectural patterns, sometimes the color and decor, or possibly the road sign or the symbol used in the advertising. The chain operations could and did refer business to one another. They had advance registration and guaranteed reservation plans. In many cases they enjoyed nationwide advertising and sales promotion campaigns.

In order to service the independent operator, a number of referral organizations grew up in this country, and several have achieved great growth and success. Referral associations, which are organized on a non-profit basis, are owned and controlled by the members. Through this type of organization the independent is able to get sales promotion benefits similar to those enjoyed by a chain operation but without sacrificing his individual control of the business. The independent operator also becomes associated closely with other independents in the business. In addition, by belonging to a well-known referral organization, he now has the brand name image that seems so important in today's marketing. Each referral organization not only operates a reservation system but also has certain minimum standards which each motel owner, if he is to maintain his membership, must meet. His motel must periodically pass an inspection of facilities, service, standards, and character. Failure to meet these standards means loss of his membership in the association and his identification with this organization. Each member pays annual dues and may also be subject to advertising assessments, usually based on so much per room per day with a maximum daily total. The dues ordinarily run according to the size of the motel.

Among the referral associations some of the best known are Alamo Plaza, Best Western, Best Eastern, Master Hosts, Superior Motels, Emmons Walker, Congress of Motor Hotels, and America's Best Choice. This list is certainly not complete, but is representative of the referral organizations that have sprung up in this country.

The most rapid development in the entire industry in recent years has been the growth of franchising. Franchising is not new —Howard Johnson has been using it for years with his restaurants. However, it was during the 1950's that franchising came into its own with regard to the motel and motor hotel business.

Many of the very best customers of franchise operations do not realize the difference between a chain operation and an independent franchise operation. The appearance, layout, room furnishings, and, to a great extent, the menu are standardized. The only real difference is in the financial arrangements, and these are not known to the customer. Under a franchising system many an individual has an opportunity to go into business for himself and at the same time has a ready helping hand to assist him at any and all times. For example, let's say that an individual in city Z is very much interested in getting into the motel business and has a piece of property that he feels would be a fine location. He approaches one of the franchise organizations to make a proper business arrangement. Ordinarily he would pay a license fee to the organization as well as some type of daily fee per room for advertising and would lease the sign to be used in front of the motel. For his investment he will now, in turn, receive assistance in architectural planning, and he may well be directed to mortgage lenders. In many cases the feasibility study—as well as assistance in training his staff, developing accounting procedures, purchasing procedures, and general standard operating procedures—will be given to him by the franchise organization. He will benefit from the referral system of the franchise chain as well as from the national advertising. In some cases he will be able to purchase equipment and supplies through a subsidiary owned by the franchise chain. Such central buying can save a considerable amount of money.

Among the very well known franchise chains in this country are Congress Inns, Downtowner, Holiday Inns, Howard Johnson's, Hyatt House, Albert Pick, Quality Courts, Ramada Inns, Sheraton Inns, Hilton, and Stuckey's. With the exception of Sheraton, Albert Pick, and Holiday Inns, the franchise chain does not own and operate properties of its own. Sheraton and Albert Pick are large and famous hotel companies with holdings in different parts of the country; thus they do have many operations which are wholly owned and operated by the company. The great majority of the Holiday Inns in this country are franchise operations, but there is a small number of Holiday Inns operated by the parent company out of Memphis.

Franchising has been a great boon to the individual investor who wanted to go into business for himself. Even though he has all the benefits of a chain operation, a franchise owner is, in the long run, an independent operator—his own boss. The benefits of franchising to the operator have already been mentioned. A student of the industry might wonder, however, why a nationally known hotel organization such as Sheraton or Hilton would want to risk its fine name and reputation by entering the franchise field. While it is true that any franchise organization has high standards and constantly surveys the franchise operation to see that these standards are maintained, it still does not have the same degree of control over quality, cleanliness, and service that it would have in its own self-operated organization. Since more and more large companies are entering the field, there have to be advantages that outweigh these disadvantages. In the first place, franchising provides an opportunity for an organization to spread its name rapidly and widely throughout the country at a minimum amount of expense. Second, not only do the franchise operations benefit from the hotel's name and referral system, but also act as booking agents for the hotels of the organization. The referral business thus becomes a two-way street and the various franchise operations may be excellent sources of rooms and food and beverage business for the metropolitan hotels. Third, a hotel knows that its name is worth money. Franchising makes it worth a great deal of money. Since every franchisee pays a franchise fee and a daily charge to the organization, there is plenty of money to be made in franchising. This opportunity to make money has to be one of the major reasons for hotel companies entering the franchise field.

There is one other arrangement fairly common in the field, called Co-Owner Chain. Here the motel is owned in partnership between the parent company and the local investor. The local investor usually owns about 50 percent of the stock of the motel, the parent corporation owns the remainder. It is the parent corporation which selects the site, designs, finances, builds, and furnishes the motel and supervises the operation. The most famous of the co-owner chains is Travel Lodge.

ADOPTION OF BUSINESS MANAGEMENT TECHNIQUES

During the greater part of hotelkeeping history, emphasis has been on the hosting or showmanship qualities of managerial talent. Although the industry has been necessarily operated on a general business basis, there has not been the need for the application of new techniques that were developing rapidly in other businesses. Many operators felt that the hotel business was unique and that management methods that were successfully utilized in other industries were not applicable to hotel operations. Thus, while business organizations were undergoing revolutionary changes and developments, the hotel industry continued to operate in much the same manner it had since the turn of the century. The industry, without realizing the situation, was falling more and more behind most business organizations in its management methods and approaches. Slowly the lag began to take its toll and was revealed in the approach to the myriad problems that suddenly confronted the hotel operator. Operating costs skyrocketed, occupancy figures nosedived, employees became harder to attract and even more difficult to retain as turnover figures became unbelievably high. The unions entered the field with new vigor and new success, and profits shrank or disappeared. Management needed solutions to these problems. Being a good host just wasn't the approach to provide them.

It was during the 1950's that hotel management began to explore modern management techniques. Adoption came rapidly and was accelerated in the 1950's. The first impetus came from the chain organizations but has spread rapidly to the independents.

Today's hotel manager is knee-deep in data processing, studying computer adoption to hotels, and working with precost and precontrol of food and beverage. His interest in employer-employee relations has been kindled and he is working constantly with payroll control systems, budgets, unit labor costs, percentages, and statistics. He has learned that there is such a thing as marketing and market analysis and, most importantly, that the hotel business has a genuine need for them.

Research into every phase of hotel management is encouraged by the Statler Foundation and is being carried out at Cornell's School of Hotel Administration. From research will come answers that will refine and improve the new business techniques.

The adoption of business management techniques and the rush to make up for lost time has greatly increased the demand for college-trained men in hotel executive ranks. Though Cornell opened its school in 1922 and graduated its first class in 1925, the demand through the 1930's and 1940's was not overpowering. The Cornell graduate had no trouble finding a position, but he and his colleagues were only then establishing firmly the influence of the college man in the hotel industry. Because of the caliber and demonstrated ability of these men and the need for men trained in modern management, by 1950 the demand far exceeded the supply and has continued thus right to the present day. The number of four-year colleges offering hotel management has grown to nine, and junior colleges having this as a subject have sprung up all over the country.

Hotel management has come of age as a profession that demands a detailed knowledge of science and management techniques. The future will see an ever-increasing demand for intelligent, educated young people in our industry.

Increased Importance of Food and Beverage

Until the close of World War I there were few steakhouses or specialty restaurants in this country. In the large cities, hotels handled most of the food business. Then came prohibition. Hotels could no longer serve liquor, so guests sought out the local speakeasy. At first such places served only drinks, but soon the owners realized that people liked to eat while they drank. Starting with sandwiches, the speak-easy operator branched out into full course meals as a service to his clientele. It is interesting to note that many famous restaurants like "21," Lindy's, and El Morocco started as speak-easies. By the time prohibition was repealed the habit of dining at the local speak-easy was so ingrained in the average customer that he continued the practice, and hotels have never won back the food business they lost in 1919.

That the hotel industry is starting to counterattack becomes more evident every day. Hotels have varied their restaurants so that a guest may obtain anything from a snack to a full course meal with French service and can find a menu to fit any budget.

THE ROLE OF FOOD AND BEVERAGE IN HOTELS

Through most of the first half of the twentieth century, food and beverage occupied a minor position of importance in the minds of many hotel operators. In some cases it was treated as a necessary evil—a service to be available just in case the guest should desire it. From an economic standpoint, the emphasis was to attempt to break even, if possible, or to lose as little as possible. At the same time there was an emphasis on quality of both food and service. The chief emphasis was on the rooms because this was where the money was. As long as one could fill the guest rooms, the profit figures on food and beverage were relatively unimportant.

During the 1950's this whole concept changed and changed radically. A number of factors influenced this change. Perhaps the most important one was the growth and expansion of motels and motor hotels. The motel hit the hotel where it hurt the most —in the sale of rooms. As motel occupancy grew, hotel occupancy declined. This occupancy decline was reflected in the profit and loss statements of the hotels. Profits diminished and the financial pinch was on. To aggravate matters further, almost every cost of operation started an upward spiral. The profit squeeze was on and management undertook a serious re-evaluation of the entire operation.

To continue to operate the food and beverage operation at break-even or at a small loss was a luxury that could no longer be afforded. The small hotel operator was the hardest hit because the motel hit him the hardest. Much of his rooms business was gone, never to return. If he were to continue his operation, it would be necessary to develop other sources of sales and profit. The alternative was to close his doors and be replaced by a parking lot or some other use of the land his hotel now occupied.

Were there profits to be made in food and beverage? The answer appeared to be affirmative. After all, restaurants had made money for years and their only source of income was food sales or food and beverage sales. First must come a change of image. When the average citizen considered "eating out," he seldom thought of going to a hotel dining room. In his opinion it was "expensive," "too high class," and besides, he rationalized, the food wasn't very good anyway. Consequently, he patronized the restaurants.

Hotels have worked hard to change this image and, fortunately, have met with success. It was soon realized that the consumer demanded a variety of choices in types of establishments when he ate out. A rapid service coffee shop, a snack bar, a cocktail lounge with a distinctive atmosphere, a specialty restaurant built on a theme. The traditional, formal hotel dining room was obsolete.

Today the coffee shop is standard and the specialty rooms are thriving. Perhaps the most spectacular success has been the

Trader Vic restaurants featured in many Hilton hotels. Marriott has enjoyed great success with its Kona Kai and Sheraton often features the Kon Tiki restaurants. The Hotel Corporation of America features the Rib Room and came up with a real merchandising coup when it featured a room where whiskey is sold by the pound. Specialty steak houses and even key clubs are common in hotels today. It is interesting to note that in almost every case the entrance to the restaurant is directly from the street. In many cases the customer does not even realize that the restaurant is associated with or operated by the hotel. The fact that it is no longer necessary to traipse through the lobby to the restaurant is very sound from the social viewpoint. No longer is food and beverage business tolerated by management; it is promoted, merchandised, and sold through sound planning and procedures.

Hotels have made tremendous strides in increasing food and beverage sales, but there are still battles to be won. Most analyses of hotel guest eating habits reveal that a majority of the guests eat breakfast in the hotel, fewer have lunch there, and dinner attracts the smallest number. From a financial viewpoint, hotels would like to reverse the figures because, generally speaking, dinner is the most profitable meal, followed by luncheon, with breakfast the least profitable.

Changing the image and attracting new business was only half the battle. If the food operation sustained a loss, increasing the number of patrons merely increased the loss. Food and beverage departments had to be put on a profit basis, and this meant a complete overhaul of standards and procedures. The chain operations were the leaders and the pioneers. Every facet was analyzed, every procedure closely scrutinized. Most importantly, new ideas and methods were instituted. Purchasing and receiving standards and specifications were developed, various pre-cost and pre-control systems were adopted, yield tests were conducted, forecasting became a management tool, and staffing guides were created and followed. The result has been a much prettier picture on the financial statements.

Any manager will tell you that making a profit on food is difficult and requires scientific procedures and experience that one does not acquire quickly or easily. In the field today there is a tremendous demand for trained and experienced food and beverage men. The demand far exceeds the supply and the salaries are excellent. In addition, the pathway to top management is wide open for executives with a sound food and beverage background. Though national figures still show room sales as the number one source of revenue, many a hotel today produces more food and beverage revenue than rooms revenue. Each year food and beverage inches upward its share of total hotel income.

GROWTH OF CHAIN OPERATION

Chain operation is not new to the hotel industry. Operation of several hotels by one organization has been a common practice for over fifty years, but until recently the number of hotels under chain control represented a small minority of the total industry. The tremendous growth of chains gained momentum during the last years of World War II and immediately after. It was then that the three major chains—Statler, Hilton, and Sheraton— began to grow rapidly. The conservative Statler group built the Washington and Los Angeles Statlers and started construction in Dallas and Hartford. Hilton and Sheraton decided the quicker method of growth was to purchase existing hotels. Both groups bought and sold properties so rapidly that a score card was needed to keep up with the transactions. Both Hilton and Sheraton were referred to as real estate brokers rather than hotel operators. Whether the charges were justified or not is now of no consequence; both groups have long since proved that they are in the business to operate first class properties.

The largest financial transaction in the history of the hotel industry reduced the Big Three to the Big Two. Statler hotels had long been recognized as the best operated and most profitable hotels in the country. For years a good percentage of the profits had been ploughed back into the business, with the result that the company was worth much more than the listed value of the stock. Stockholders sought a means of getting their money out of the company. Management could have declared large dividends, but most stockholders would have been subject to high income taxes and the government would have reaped most of the benefits; also, the stockholder would have retained but twenty-five cents of each dollar of dividends. The only method of retaining a fair share of the money was to sell the corporation. Profits thus realized would then be long-term capital gains and would be subject to lower tax rates. When the company was put on the market Statler stock was selling at approximately twenty-four dollars a share. Mr. William Zeckendorf of Webb and Knapp—a national real estate company—went to the management of the Statler Corporation and worked out an arrangement whereby he would buy the stock for fifty dollars a share. Press releases and publicity had the deal practically consummated, but what everyone had overlooked was the intense interest of Conrad Hilton in the Statler chain. While Zeckendorf dealt with management, Hilton, through his chief representative Mr. Joseph Binns, concentrated on the stockholders. Many interesting stories of how the final deal was resolved have been told. The important fact, however, is that the Hotels Statler Corporation was sold to Mr. Hilton for approximately fifty dollars a share, or fifty million dollars. With this purchase the Hilton Corporation became the largest hotel chain the world has ever known.

Although the two giants, Hilton and Sheraton, have had the greatest volume growth, many other chains exist and they too are adding properties to their holdings. Space does not permit a detailed listing of all chains but several of the more prominent are: Albert Pick Hotels, Knott Hotels, Hotel Corporation of America, Marriott Motor Hotels, Schimmel Hotels, Western International Hotels, Intercontinental Hotels, American Hotels Corporation, Loews Hotels, Treadway Inns, Dinkler Hotels, and Jack Tarr Hotels.

Why has chain operation experienced such a tremendous growth? The best one word answer would be *efficiency*. When faced with stiff competition from efficient chain operation an independent hotel operator had three alternatives. He could try to compensate for the decline in business by cutting down maintenance expenditures and forcing up room rates. This approach was popular but suicidal. If the individual had the capital, he could gamble and invest it in improvements, modernization, and promotion. This approach was sound and has kept many hotels independent. The third recourse was to sell out in hopes of making some profit before it was too late. This is the reason why the chain operators were able to expand without engaging in a great deal of new construction.

Mr. Ernest Henderson, President of the Sheraton Corporation of America, has cited the chief advantages of chain operation:

"There are great opportunities for capitalizing group action as a means of increasing business and reducing duplication, inefficiency, and waste.

"The principal advantages of chain—over independent—hotelkeeping include these:

"Purchasing—by buying anything from foodstuffs to furniture in huge volume, a chain will enjoy substantial discounts.

"Personnel—a chain can better afford top specialists in every phase of hotel operation—engineers, food controllers, decorators, architectural planners, accountants, sales experts—simply by spreading the expense over its many units. Few single hotels can afford such specialization.

"Promotion—national advertising campaigns in magazines and newspapers are generally prohibitive for single hotels; but they can be most profitable when the expense is divided among

41 hotels, each reaping full benefit of national coverage at a fraction of the total cost.

"Reservations—free teletype reservation service permits a chain to channel, if not refer direct, business to the various hotels in the group. As about one fourth of all room reservations are made through such service, this obviously puts considerable trade out of reach of independent hotels.

"Financing—a group finds it somewhat easier to raise all-important capital for improvement or expansion, for underwriters can better appraise a financial risk by studying the present and past effectiveness of a chain's corporate management."

Because of competitive pressure by chains, the independent operator faced the greatest challenge of his career. The small community hotel faced a double challenge—the efficiency of chain operation and the competition of the motel industry, which had already made heavy inroads into his rooms business. Caught in this cross fire, and because his survival was directly dependent upon his ability to adjust to this new situation, the independent community hotelman was forced to change his mode of operation. To remain in business he had to increase food and beverage revenue to counteract the decline in room revenue.

The large, first-class independent hotels counterattacked the chains. Jealous of their independence and rightfully proud of their reputation for fine service, they sought various means of gaining certain advantages of chain operation with no sacrifice of their autonomy. This attitude is exemplified in "Distinguished Hotels." The Robert Warner Agency persuaded several famous independent hotels to pool their resources for advertising, promotion, and reservation service. Working as a group, the hotels are able to match the efficiency of chain operation in these three areas, but they are careful to point out that Distinguished Hotels is not a chain. The future will undoubtedly see an expansion and a refinement of such techniques.

The growth and expansion of chain operation may have

reached a peak in the late 1950's and early 1960's, but it certainly has not stopped. For example, when this book was first published in 1958 there was no chain of Loews Hotels. Today they operate six properties in New York City alone. The nature and type of the hotels in the recent expansion has changed somewhat. Hilton has built a number of inns at airport locations and in other areas. A great number of both Hilton Inns and Sheraton Inns have appeared recently, are under construction, or are at least on the drawing board. Many of the most recent Hilton and Sheraton Inns are franchise operations but still must be classified generally as chain-operated hotels.

From the decrease in independent hotels has come the prediction that within a few years the independent hotel will no longer exist. However, there are too many excellent medium and large independents for such a thing to happen. Among the famous independent hotels of the country are The Pierre, The Essex House, The Carlisle and The Tuscany in New York, The Drake Hotel in Chicago, The Muhlebach in Kansas City, St. Louis' Chase-Park Plaza, Denver's Brown Palace, The Fairmont and Mark Hopkins in San Francisco, The Warwick in Houston and the Ambassador in Los Angeles.

Boom or Bust

With a history of boom and bust, the stability and financial solvency of the hotel industry are viewed somewhat apprehensively by investors. In reality, there have been only the two great boom periods: the twenties and the mid-fifties to mid-sixties; the one terrible depression occurred in 1929. The recent boom in building has not been accompanied by a boom in the amount of business done and this has caused considerable concern in ownership and management circles. Are we badly overbuilt? Are we headed for a real depression that could well wipe out the industry? These are difficult questions to answer.

Certainly the industry has a much firmer financial base than it did in 1929. Forecasts for business in general are favorable. The standard of living continues to improve and the discretionary income of the American family increases each year. At the same time, the latter part of the 1960's is a period of financial strain. Occupancy is low, costs are high, and profits very small. A number of famous hotels are disappearing from the scene along with many lesser known properties. For example, in New York City alone The Astor Hotel has closed its doors; already demolished are The Park Lane, The Savoy Plaza, and The New Weston, and The Sheraton East, formerly The Ambassador, is scheduled for demolition. In all fairness, it should be pointed out that not all these properties failed as hotels, but rather as investments. The land they occupied was so valuable that the hotels simply could not earn a fair return on the investment. In most cases, these hotels will be replaced by office buildings.

What does the future hold? My crystal ball is a little hazy. Perhaps the best answer comes from a recent article in *Forbes Magazine*. The authors conclude, "Those who say that in five or ten years hotels will boom again probably are over-optimistic; those who say they will never boom again, though some hotels and motels will continue to make money, probably are too pessimistic. The only really safe statement to make is this: in the long run the chains will probably become quite profitable again. But even this prediction must be hedged. They will prosper again, *provided* they manage their affairs well in the critical days just ahead."

AMERICAN RESORT HOTELS

While hotelmen concentrated their heaviest efforts on accommodations for the *traveling* public, they did not neglect the vacation-minded American. Although there were resorts in colonial America, the real development of the American resort hotel came with the expansion of the railways. The luxury resort developed in the

South after the Civil War—The Greenbrier at White Sulphur Springs, West Virginia, and The Homestead at Hot Springs, Virginia, were among the earliest. At this period thousands of people yearly began to be attracted to the many spas and mineral springs across the country, so it was only natural that large resort hotels should locate in areas where these were most common. Saratoga in New York State is an excellent example of this type of resort area; Warm Springs, Georgia, is another. As transportation facilities developed, hotels were opened along the seashore and in the mountains. Traditionally the resort hotel was a summer operation, and in addition to providing comfortable rooms and excellent cuisine it offered a location with scenic, historical, recreational, or therapeutic advantages.

The winter resort—generally a hotel located in an equable year-round climate—was a later development and did not catch the public's fancy until the opening of the twentieth century. By then the automobile was becoming a practical means of travel, and it made more accessible areas of the country where the climate was ideal for wintertime vacationing. As one instance, golf had become a popular American pastime, and the enticement of year-round golf served to attract even more people to these places.

California was the first region to develop as a winter resort area. In fact, the early rapid growth of Los Angeles was a direct result of that city's popularity as a resort center. Florida, on the other hand, developed more slowly. Atlhough Henry Fagler opened the Ponce de Leon Hotel in St. Augustine in 1885, Florida's real development as a resort did not get under way until 1910. By 1920 Florida had surpassed California as the nation's winter vacationland, and from 1920 to the present the heaviest concentration of resort hotels in this country has been in and around Miami. Today California and Florida reign as the two leading wintertime vacation areas; however, during the past few years the Southwest has shown definite indications of becoming an active winter recreation region.

Arizona is the foremost resort area of the Southwest, and the cities of Phoenix and Tucson are its principal centers. The region has great natural attractions, its winter season is warm and sunny, and its climate is clear and dry. The exceptionally dry weather has been a dominant reason for attracting residents from all over the nation because of its health benefits. In recent years, however, the health seekers have been augmented by the fun-loving, sun-worshiping set.

It is difficult to classify or categorize resorts because of the tremendous variations existing among them. Generally speaking, resorts fall into the four categories of summer resort, warm winter resort, cold winter resort, and year-round resort.

The summer resort operates during late May, June, July, August, and through Labor Day or possibly into early October. The traditional social season is July Fourth to Labor Day. The northeastern section of the United States is probably the largest summer resort area of the country. Minnesota, Wisconsin, Michigan, Arkansas, and parts of the Rocky Mountain area also feature summer resorts. In the Northeast, New England is a famous resort area featuring seashore resorts and mountain resorts. New York State is famous for its Adirondack and Catskill Mountain areas; Pennsylvania features the Pocono Mountains. The Atlantic Coast from northern New Jersey to North Carolina is dotted with resorts and blessed with many beautiful sandy beaches.

The resort business in general is a very volatile, hazardous occupation and perhaps the most hazardous of all is summer resort operation. The season is short (ten to twelve weeks at best) and the operator is at the mercy of the elements. A week of rain, cool weather, the threat of a hurricane—any of these factors will start a mass exodus from the resorts. Should this happen during a week in which the resort has a full house, it could easily change a profit into a loss for the year.

When this book was first published in 1958, I predicted that within fifteen years as many as 75% of the summer resorts then in operation might well be closed. To say that the prediction created a stir in resort circles would be the understatement of the year. The prediction was qualified by the statement that this would happen *unless* the operators took a close look at their operations and began to change and modernize in keeping with the realities of the second half of the twentieth century. The handwriting was on the wall, the trend was already established. Unfortunately, not enough of the owners were reading it and some were doomed no matter what measures they took, short of building an entirely new hotel.

There were and are just too many factors working against them. In the first place, many of the buildings were old and the accommodations were obsolete in the modern market. Rooms without bath, for example, are rather difficult to sell in today's market. The clientele remained static—the same people were coming back each year—and therefore it was getting older and smaller every year. Other things were happening, too. The winter vacation was becoming ever more popular and this reduced the amount of summer vacation time. The habits, tastes, and interests of the traveling public were changing rapidly and radically. The American family no longer stayed put in one spot for its vacation. To pack the family into a station wagon and roam like gypsies over a wide area was much in vogue. Now we had a horde of one-night guests and they slept in a motel more often than in a resort hotel. The whole concept of a good vacation changed. Unfortunately, the formality and tradition of the old-time resort had no role to play in this concept.

To make matters even worse, the jet age arrived and now every American resort found itself in direct competition with Europe and other glamorous areas of the world. The southern winter resorts became year-round operations and siphoned off more customers; still another segment of the public discovered camping. The summer resort operator faced the greatest challenge of his career and not every one was able to meet it.

One should not reach the conclusion that all summer resorts are doomed. A number are thriving. It is really a case of the rich getting richer and the poor getting poorer. To their credit, many owners and operators are battling to stay in business and to meet the demands of the new market. In New England we find a tremendous promotion in The Heritage Trail, which ties together history and resorts. Off to a somewhat shaky start, it now is developing beautifully and is building business for its supporters.

Other summer operations suddenly found themselves right in the heart of a developing ski area. A whole new world of opportunity presented itself. Now they had a winter season, too, and business was plentiful. These lucky people now have money to refurbish rooms and upgrade and modify their properties. In reality, however, these operations are no longer summer resorts in the true sense of the word.

The resorts operating year-round enjoyed success and profit through the fifties and sixties. They too found their markets changing but somehow managed to stay with the times. Most importantly they were building a new young clientele to replace the ever-dwindling old-time population.

As late as the mid-1950's, many hotelmen thought the mania for skiing was a limited development, and one which had little to offer a resort operator. In those days, the ski enthusiast had little money and was interested primarily in reasonable accommodations, no matter how crowded they might be. Many a wise old financial expert cautioned not to invest in ski lodges. There was even a saying, "Unfortunately, bankers don't ski." A few pioneers went right ahead anyway and soon found themselves in possession of a gold mine. The ski craze grew and grew. People with plenty of money took up the sport and the cold winter resort had a genuine boom on its hands. New ski slopes were building hotels and, just as importantly, older hotels were developing ski slopes. Skiing was "in" for everyone from ski bum to the jet setter. As is so true with many sports, as many came to watch and to be seen as came to ski. They all needed hospitality services, however, and to complete the resort man's joy, had money to pay and did not seem to be very price conscious.

The greatest growth of all came in the warm winter resort area. The lure of the hot sun, golden beaches, and gay night life is overpowering when one peers out his window in subzero temperatures to see snow driven by gale force winds piling up in his driveway. No wonder the winter vacation grows in popularity each year. The growth of Miami Beach is one of the success stories of the post war period. Less than fifty years ago Miami had 5 hotels and 12 apartments. Today it boasts over 400 hotels with about 38,000 guest rooms. The city has 48 hotels per square mile. One hundred hotels with 100 rooms or more have been built in Miami since the end of World War II.

But even Florida sometimes can be cold and cloudy. The winter vacationer wants the sun guaranteed. He must return to the office or the job with today's number-one status badge—a suntan. Just a little south of Florida, man is guaranteed heat and sun. The hotel growth and development in the Carribbean nearly defies description. Madison Avenue's most flamboyant adjectives are not sufficient. Jamaica, Barbados, Puerto Rico, the Virgin Islands, Nassau, and Trinidad. Tropical paradises featuring the world's most modern (in some cases) hotels and only a few hours from any metropolitan center in the United States. Winter is the big season—one need only look at the rates to be convinced—but more and more the islands are attracting summer business as well. As in Florida, the summer clientele is entirely different socially and economically. What this group may lack in money, it more than makes up in volume. Not only has jet travel made the trip convenient and reasonable, but the airlines are continually promoting vacations in the sun.

The greatest resort story of the postwar period has to be the development of Hawaii. Blessed with an ideal year-round climate, Hawaii has a twelve-month season. Most famous of the islands is Oahu, with Honolulu, Waikiki Beach and such famous and familiar hotels as the Royal Hawaiian, Moana, Surf Rider, and Princess Kaikulani. Oahu has no space left for building and the outer islands seem to be hatching hotels. Every major United

States chain has at least one hotel in Hawaii and several have two or more. As is true of the Carribbean, Hawaii is deeply indebted to the jet airplane for much of its popularity and success.

Two other developments have played a major role in the resort business of the postwar years. One is a replay on an old theme and the other exploits a new one. As stated earlier, many of the early resorts grew up around the natural spas, and health restoration was a primary motive of many of the guests. However, in the postwar years changes occurred and the spas became less and less attractive. A few of the old-timers continued to return each year, but the figures on spa resorts occupancy continued to dwindle.

In the early sixties, the American public suddenly became quite health conscious once again. A new emphasis on physical fitness was generated by publicity concerning the number of young people rejected by the draft as physically unfit. The heavy toll of heart deaths was related in many instances to overweight. Medical discoveries on cholesterol contributed to an increasing diet consciousness on the part of the American public. To a few enterprising hoteliers, these factors pointed out a new opportunity. Health resorts were opened. These resorts offered all the usual resort services, but in addition featured special diet meals, exercise and physical fitness under expert guidance, and a small medical staff to provide the guest with a vacation that would increase his physical fitness. Originating in Florida, these health resorts may be found in significant numbers on the east coast and in some other areas of the country. The prognosis is for continued growth in this type operation. It is conceivable that with modifications and modernization, many of the older spa resorts may enjoy a rejuvenation.

Faced with declining occupancy, increased costs of operation and profits turning to losses, seasonal resorts desperately sought sources of new business to augment the income from the regular social season. Attempts to lengthen the social season by opening earlier or closing later met with little success. The weather was not good, but most importantly, the guests would not change their vacation habits. Unable to extend the social season, the resorts sought other business that might occupy these early and late season periods.

Fortunately, resorts discovered conventions, and for a great many of them it has been the key to salvation. In many respects, a resort is an ideal location of a convention—especially a working convention. More and more, the emphasis is on serious work, discussion, and education; the good-time social factor is soft-pedaled. The resort offers recreation and relaxation but is removed from the bright lights and multitude of distractions to be found in any metropolitan area. As a result, each year shows an increase in conventions held at resorts.

While convention business has been a bonanza to many resorts, it does create some problems. Social guests do not appreciate convention groups and there are times when the convention season overlaps the social season. In discussing this problem with one operator, he admitted that it was a touchy situation and one that might lose some regular guests. When a guest complains, he tries to point out diplomatically that without the convention business there would be no resort and thus no social season to enjoy.

Exact figures on dollar volume of conventions held at resorts are not available. It is a known fact, however, that in many a resort today, the major source of income is convention business. The Greenbrier, certainly one of the nation's very finest resorts, was not a great financial success for quite a period. Under the leadership of E. Truman Wright, the facilities were remodeled and designed for convention business. Today, The Greenbrier is one of the leading convention hotels in the country. Without the change to facilities for conventions, it could very readily be a mammoth white elephant. The owner of one of New England's famous summer resort hotels has stated that today 70 percent of his total sales come from conventions. For further proof, one need only look at Atlantic City. The famous boardwalk hotels that for years were gay social centers and the summer residences for the wealthy could not possibly survive today without convention business. Even the famous mountain resorts typified by world-famous Grossingers are now very active in the convention field. Had not resorts discovered and attracted conventions, many a famous vacation spot today would be only a fond memory.

International Expansion

In the first edition of this book, the author pointed out four basic trends that were developing in the international hotelkeeping field. They were (1) an increasing awareness on the part of more and more countries of the monetary value of tourist business, (2) a growing boom in international hotelkeeping, (3) the increasing dominance of the American hotel management influence throughout the world, and (4) an increase in American operation of and investment in foreign hotels. Each of these trends is today a well-established fact.

The tourism boom has reached such proportions as to seem almost unbelievable to many people. Countries of the world realize that tourism offers the opportunity to earn hard money with no expenditure of natural resources. Though the hotels are the direct beneficiaries of tourism, the other parts of the economy are bolstered by it. Reliable estimates reveal that for every dollar spent in hotels by a tourist, he spends three dollars in the community. Little wonder then that governments are actively promoting travel and tourism in their countries.

Up-to-date travel statistics are impossible to obtain. There is usually a lag of two years in their publication. Nevertheless, Table 5 (World Travel Statistics) will illustrate the tremendous growth in tourism. Impressive as these figures are, they under-estimate the current travel and tourism picture. The increase between 1964 and 1967 was even sharper. To provide the reader with a view based on money is possible only through the year 1964. In

TABLE 5   World Travel Statistics

	Visitor Arrivals 1960	Visitor Arrivals 1964	% Increase 1964 over 1960
Europe	50,351,156	79,097,082	+ 57
North America	15,197,741	18,074,997	+ 19
Latin America and Caribbean	2,705,494	3,326,677	+ 23
Middle East	1,380,152	2,258,212	+ 59
Asia and Australia	863,635	2,032,945	+135
Africa	430,917	1,633,876	+300
Totals	70,929,095	106,423,789	+ 52

Source: *Cornell Hotel and Restaurant Administration Quarterly*

1964 tourist receipts were $10,143,500,000 and that is a considerable sum of money even in today's inflated economy.

Of all nationalities, the American for years has been the world's greatest traveler. Although challenged by the Germans, he still maintains the number one position in the world. In 1960, 2,001,624 Americans traveled to overseas countries. By 1965 the number had increased to 3,341,086, which is an increase of 67 percent in five years. Where do Americans travel? The best answer is "everywhere": 1,392,213 of them traveled to Europe, 269,185 visited Asia, another 16,154 explored Africa, and 51,197 even travelled "down under" to Oceania. North and Central America were very popular, attracting 1,185,984; 93,104 visited South America. Short or extended sea voyages were in favor, too —333,249 went on a cruise.

It is interesting to note the areas which showed the greatest percentage increase in American visitors. In order they were Asia, Oceania, and cruise. Europe still attracts a huge number, but one sees the trend to other areas of the world or other areas within Europe. Switzerland, Greece, Portugal, Ireland, and Spain produced Europe's largest increases. In Asia it was Israel, Japan, and Hong Kong. Central America found both Jamaica and the Netherlands West Indies nearly tripling the number of visiting Americans between 1960 and 1965.

There can be no doubt of the tourism boom, which displays no sign of dissipating in the near future. That the American management concept is now the dominant one throughout the world seems to be no longer open to question. For example, Cornell's School of Hotel Administration has, upon request, conducted hotel management seminars on every continent of the world except Antarctica and that is the exceptional area that has not increased greatly its tourist business. Giving increased credence to this dominance is the presence of 70 international students, representing 35 different countries, in the student body of the School. Each summer, additional international students are attracted to the summer session.

American hotel companies continue to expand their influence internationally. In the international field we find the familiar names of Hilton, Sheraton, Hotel Corporation of America, Western International, and Knott. The pioneer of them all, however, is Intercontinental Hotels. Early to recognize the relationship between air travel and hotel accommodations, Pan American Airways formed Intercontinental Hotels as a wholly owned subsidiary. Hotels were built along the Pan American air routes. While the early growth was primarily in Central and South America, Intercontinental has more recently expanded around the world. The corporation currently has 38 hotels in operation with 12 more in the planning stage. Hilton International Hotels encircle the globe and currently number 41. Sheraton has operated in Canada for many years, but only in recent years has the company ventured farther afield. With hotels in Israel, Venezuela, the Philippines, and Japan, Sheraton has now joined the international picture in earnest. Western International is also expanding very rapidly in Central and South America, Mexico, and the Pacific area.

Most of the American-operated international hotels utilize

the management contract concept of operation. The actual hotel is built, financed, and owned by individuals, companies, or organizations within the country. The American hotel company furnishes capital and management for the hotel and for this service receives a set fee or a percentage of the gross sales. A system is worked out to share profits between the owners and the management company. Since the management contract concept requires little capital, the international company may expand rapidly. Up until now, the international competition was between the new American-owned hotel and the local national hotel. With the continued expansion, the American companies will soon be competing with each other in many parts of the world.

What is the market for these shiny new hotels in all parts of the world? Certainly the American traveler is a prime prospect, but each of these hotels has its eye on a totally cosmopolitan market. To the American, a Hilton, Sheraton Intercontinental, or a Western is a touch of home—an oasis in the midst of strange and exotic surroundings. He is usually not proficient in languages and he knows he will have no language problem in an American-operated hotel. It is fun for him to explore the customs, habits, and traditions of a foreign country, but when evening arrives he wants his accommodations American style, for that is what he is accustomed to. Let us be completely objective. The American loves his hot dogs, hamburgers, milk shakes, and ice water. They are a touch of home and they are available in the American hotel. In summary, the American hotel offers familiarity, a feeling of security, high standards of sanitation, decor, and service as well as a new, modern building with the most modern of fixtures and equipment.

The American-operated hotel is achieving success in attracting the other nationals too. In the first place, it does not advertise that it is an American hotel. The image sought is that of a modern international hotel with a flavoring of local atmosphere. While it may not excel its local competition in every facet of hospitality, it holds enough superiority to attract the discerning and affluent world traveler. Perhaps most importantly, it has served as motivation for the local hotels to upgrade and modernize their facilities.

CHAPTER 2

The Industry in Perspective

The profession of hotel management is one of the most challenging, and at the same time little understood, occupations in the American economy. Although most communities of any size have one or more hotels, and although the average citizen has had some contact with at least one during his lifetime, very few people realize the diversfied knowledge, the variety of skills, and the ingenuity demanded of the successful hotel manager.

Webster defines a hotel as "a building or institution providing lodging, meals, and service for the public." It is my intent throughout this book to give you insight into the behind-the-scenes activity, the organization, and the cooperation that are necessary in producing the services expected by the public, with the hope that you will gain a clear concept of the hotel industry.

SIZE AND SCOPE OF THE INDUSTRY

Hotels are to be found in every country of the world, in any city with a population of over 10,000, and, very commonly, in places with fewer than 500 inhabitants. It is no wonder that hotelkeeping ranks high among the largest worldwide industries. Although there are no reliable world statistics or figures available, an overall view of the industry as it exists in the United States should provide a good picture of the magnitude of this business.

In America, hotelkeeping is the seventh-ranking service industry, coming after only such giants as public transportation and restaurant management. In America, there are approximately 22,100 hotels, with a total of 1,300,000 rooms. American hotels can accommodate over 2,000,000 guests each night of the year and can offer dining facilities for over 1,000,000 people. Total hotel receipts are presently about $3,190,000,000 per year, and hotels have an annual payroll expense of $1,300,000,000. When we hear or read about a hotel, it is usually some eminent hotel in a well-known metropolitan area: Chicago's Conrad Hilton, with its 3,000 rooms, New York's Waldorf-Astoria, with its 47 stories and famous towers, and San Francisco's Sheraton Palace Hotel, a distinctive landmark. However, even though the large and famous hotels play an important part in American life, they are not typical of the hotel industry in the United States or in the world. Only 6 percent of all American hotels have over 300 rooms, and 70 percent have fewer than 100 rooms; the remaining 24 percent range in size between 100 and 300 rooms. Thus we are dealing with an industry that is tremendous in overall size and scope, but whose backbone is the small businessman with his 50- to 100-room hotel.

Traditionally, the hotel industry has been one of individual ownership, and because of the average hotel's size, an individual businessman has been able to finance a hotelkeeping operation and keep ownership and management united. In recent years, skyrocketing costs have resulted in a trend toward corporate ownership, yet even today the majority of hotels are individually owned. This is evidenced by the latest available statistics, which show that 50 percent of all American hotels are under individual proprietorship, 20 percent are under partnerships, and 30 percent are under corporations. The trend toward corporate ownership has produced a new class of hotelman—the college-trained person who is choosing hotel management as a profession. In addition, absentee ownership has brought about a maze of scientific, financial, and operational systems whose intricacies and complexities can be understood and handled only by someone who has had a rather extensive educational experience. Because of this, corporate ownership of hotels has been one of the primary forces in the development of college level training in the field of hotel management.

CLASSIFICATION OF HOTELS

There are four major classifications of American hotels in the industry today: (1) the commercial or transient hotel, (2) the resort hotel, (3) the residential hotel, and (4) the motel-motor hotel. Among the 22,000 hotels approximately 75 percent are commercial, 16 percent are resort, and 9 percent are residential. There are approximately 61,500 motels and motor hotels.

The commercial hotel directs its appeal primarily to the individual traveling for business reasons, although most commercial hotels do have some permanent guests. The advent of the chain store reduced the ranks of the traveling salesmen; to replace this business, these hotels now rely typically on executives and engineers, and more and more on the individual traveling for pleasure. The past few years have even seen a very active commercial hotel campaign for family business.

The commercial hotel guest can expect a room with its own private bath, a telephone, a radio, and often a television set at no added cost. The hotel will usually have a coffee shop serving popular-priced menus, and a dining room for those desiring a more formal atmosphere, featuring the classical cuisine and a high standard of service. In those states where it is permissible, there will be a cocktail lounge to provide the guest with beverage service. In the large metropolitan hotels, there is usually a complete nightclub room featuring name entertainment. Laundry, cleaning, pressing, and other valet services are provided, and professional medical and dental service is often available within the hotel. For the guest traveling by automobile, parking and garage facilities are available although possibly not directly under control of the hotel.

Two recent innovations of the commercial hotel are the studio-type guest room and the automobile entrance and registration desk. In the studio room the beds are so designed that during the day they are comfortable divans, thus making the regular guest room an ideal place for small business conferences. The automobile entrance is a direct result of the trend toward family travel by automobile, and of a desire to meet the competition presented by motels for this business.

The majority of resort hotels are seasonally operated and are open for either the summer or the winter season, though a number operate year-round (there is now apparent an increase in all-year activity on the part of Florida winter resorts). Resorts cater to vacationers and recreation-minded people. Although the greater share of guests spend from one week to an entire season at a resort, a resort hotel's *weekend* business often presents the difference between profit and loss for the operator. Usually located at the shore, in the mountains, or at a spa, a resort is free of the large city clamor but is still easily accessible by train or automobile.

Both summer and winter resorts offer the usual hotel service, but because their clientele is made up principally of vacationers they must provide guest entertainment. In a commercial hotel the guest seldom sees the manager and looks upon the hotel primarily as temporary headquarters while he is in the city on business or just to see the sights. The resort guest, however, expects to be treated as a member of the family and to be completely entertained right on the premises. Consequently, there exists at the resort hotel a personal relationship between guests and management, and often the staff includes a social director, a recreation director, or an entertainment director. Large resorts may even have a separate recreation department.

The residential hotel is found principally in the United States. Many Americans early developed the habit of permanent living in hotels, and this branch of the industry evolved primarily to provide for these individuals. Essentially, a residential hotel is an apartment building offering maid service, a dining room, room meal service, and possibly a cocktail lounge. The food and beverage department is usually small and exists more as a convenience for the residents than as a true source of income; some residential hotels lease their food and beverage area to an outside catering organization. Residential hotels range from the luxurious, offering full suites for families, to the moderate, offering single rooms for either young men or young women. Although they represent only a segment of the industry, these hotels nevertheless perform an important function in the American way of life.

Motels and motor hotels actually fall into two categories, similar to those of hotels. A motel may be primarily commercial or it may be a resort type operation. Motels can generally be said to provide services very similar to hotels. In fact it is no longer possible to differentiate between a new motor hotel and a hotel. The one distinguishing aspect is free parking on the premises. Few hotels can offer this feature to all guests. Though commercial travelers often patronize motels, the chief source of motel guests is the person traveling for pleasure with his family.

Another distinguishing feature of the modern motel is the swimming pool. It is doubtful that anyone would dare to build a new motel without a pool. While the guest may not use the pool —only a minority ever actually do—he will not stop at a motel that doesn't have one. His thinking does not appear to be too logical in this matter, but the area of guest preferences is noted for illogical and irrational thinking.

The large motor hotels are very active in the convention market, but to the great majority of motels conventions are of little interest and account for only a minute portion of the income.

In former years the location of motels was a distinguishing feature. Invariably they were located on the perimeter of cities and along the highways. Today they are everywhere, including center city in every major city of the United States. In resort areas they often occupy prime locations. A case in point is Atlantic City. A few years ago not one motel was even close to the famous boardwalk. Today the motels have almost overshadowed the hotels in this prime location.

THE HOTEL AND THE COMMUNITY

The relationship between a hotel and its community is best expressed by paraphrasing Calvin Coolidge's remark, "What's good for business is good for America," to, "What's good for the hotel is good for the community." Since early colonial days the growth of American hotels has directly paralleled the growth of American cities and towns. In fact, the size and comfort of a city's hotels has long been recognized as a measure of its standing and importance.

In recent years cities have become more keenly aware of the business to be gained from the traveling public. Many cities conduct active campaigns for attracting visitors, and they have learned that unless a visitor can be assured of comfortable lodging and good food he will not likely be attracted by the area's scenic or recreational capacity alone. Large cities have formed convention bureaus to attract regional and national conventions; the success of these bureaus depends upon their capacity to offer visitors sufficient and comfortable accommodations. (The role of the hotel sales department in convention promotion will be discussed in a later chapter.) Many communities have been initially hesitant about spending funds to attract visitors, because it seemed to them that the hotels would be the only businesses that would profit from such an undertaking. However, experience has proved the opposite to be true.

Convention cities receive an average of $132 in "new money" from each attending delegate; hotels receive 41 cents of each dollar, but the remaining 59 cents goes to other businesses. A breakdown of daily expenditures by a convention delegate is shown in Table 6.

Small communities also have recognized the desirability of having a good hotel. In many of the smaller cities, businessmen conduct fund-raising campaigns to finance a community hotel. These men realize a much smaller return on their investment than they could receive by placing their money in other areas, but they feel that the presence of a hotel will enhance the community and indirectly boost all local business.

Two other factors that promote the close relationship be-

TABLE 6   Convention Delegate Expenditures

Daily Expenditures	% of Total
The Hotel (Rooms and Food)	41.00
Other Restaurants	15.66
Beverages	7.49
Retail Stores	15.32
Local Transportation	4.10
Theaters	1.77
Sightseeing	1.14
Night Clubs and Sports Events	5.59
Car, Oil, Gas, Service	1.92
Other	6.01
	100.00

tween hotel and community are the architectural trends to smaller, more compact homes and the increasing shortage of domestic help. Whereas at one time large dinner parties, small dances, wedding receptions, and other group gatherings were often held in private homes, today many homes lack sufficient room and the hotel stands ready to accept any or all of these functions and to assume all the chores of planning, decorating, and serving. The shortage of domestic help has served to transplant parties from the home to the hotel and has also accelerated the American habit of eating out. It is a common sight today to see an entire family enjoying a meal in the local hotel coffee shop or dining room.

That the American public is a restless group filled with wanderlust is an established fact. And it is becoming increasingly evident that *where* Americans travel is directly dependent upon the existence of facilities to satisfy their particular needs and wants. The steamship lines, the railroads, and more recently the airlines, have recognized the need for suitable food and lodging along their routes and at their destinations, and, as a result, many of the finest hotels and restaurants are owned and operated by the transportation companies. Examples of this are Santa Fe's Harvey Houses, Pan American World Airways' Intercontinental Hotels, and Canadian National Railways' and Canadian Pacific Railroads' commercial and resort hotels in Canada.

INTERNATIONAL HOTELKEEPING

Americans traveling through Europe find a general similarity among the hotels of the continental countries. By American standards European hotels are old and possess relatively little modern equipment, and, on the average, they are smaller than ours. It is unusual to find a hotel of more than 300 rooms. But whatever the hotels may lack in modern conveniences they more than make up for by providing a more complete and a more personal service than can be found in the United States. The typical American hotel has less than one employee for every guest room; European hotels average close to two employees per guest. For many years the hotels of Switzerland have been classed as the finest in Europe, but the present-day traveler will find that food and service in Italy are equally as good, and that other European hotels have adopted new ideas more rapidly than the Swiss. All European service is extremely formal.

There are very few residential hotels on the continent. A few of the famous hotels are the Ritz and the Savoy in London, the Plaza Athenie and the Ritz in Paris, Venice's Danieli Excelsior and Rome's Excelsior, the Ritz in Madrid, and the Palace at Lausanne. Equally well known are the Grosvenor House in London, the Hotel George V in Paris, the Principe Savoya in Milan, and the El Fenin in Madrid. A few of Europe's famed resorts are Scotland's Gleneagles at Auchterarder, France's Hotel du Palais at Biarritz, Italy's Grand Duchi d'Aosta at Sestriere, and Switzerland's Palace at St. Moritz.

The hotels of Canada are comparable to those of the United States. The older hotels of Central America are patterned after those of Europe, but the newer hotels show strong American influence in their architecture, decor, and services offered. In South America the older hotels are located in the seaport cities, as the sea has been the usual approach for visitors and tourists. With the development of airlines travel and the tremendous industrial boom in certain South American countries, hotels have developed rapidly inland. As in Central America, the older hotels show a strong European influence and the new structures are unmistakably in the American style.

An analysis of present-day international hotelkeeping indicates the emergence of four basic trends:

1. More and more countries of the world are becoming aware of the dollar value of tourist business. As a result, hotels are being built at a fast pace in many foreign countries. So important is the hotel to tourist attraction that many countries

are offering tax advantages to businessmen who will construct and operate hotels. Other countries are financing construction with government money and then offering lucrative operating contracts to foreign hotel organizations.

2. There is a growing boom in international hotelkeeping. The tremendous advances made by the transportation industry enable the world traveler to cover several thousand miles as quickly and as cheaply today as he could have covered several hundred miles fifteen years ago. International travel has increased during each of the past five years and shows no indication of having reached its peak. The American resort operator in particular now realizes that he is in direct competition with the rest of the world for the trade of the vacationing American.

3. The American hotel management influence is now dominant throughout the world. We need only to glance at travel statistics to find the reason for this trend. The greatest bulk of the world traveling population consists of American tourists and vacationers. This year over half a million Americans will travel to Europe, thousands more will go to Latin America, and many others will go to the Far East. While these tourists seek foreign culture, scenery, and entertainment, they expect and demand their hotel accommodations American style. And when one considers that these people spend three billion dollars yearly in foreign countries it is not surprising that the foreign hotels are rapidly adapting the American type of hotel operation.

4. American investment in and operation of foreign hotels is increasing. This trend is not as clear-cut as the other three, but it gives strong indications of growing. The development of Intercontinental Hotels Corporation along the routes of Pan American World Airways started this movement.

Hilton International Hotels now operate hotels around the world and continue to open new properties. Hilton has even invaded Paris, both downtown and at Orly Airport. Sheraton, Knott, Hotel Corporation of America, Holiday Inns, and Ramada Inns are all now operating internationally, also.

THE NATURE OF HOTEL WORK

Advantages and Disadvantages

To gain a picture of a billion-dollar industry whose most important product is an intangible requires a high degree of imagination; yet such a picture accurately describes the hotel business. It is true that many hotel products—rooms, food, and beverage—are tangibles, but the principal factor that determines the guests' attitude toward the hotel is service received. The very nature of hotelkeeping places strong emphasis on people. Although many industries have mechanized their operations and functions, ruling out the human element wherever possible, the hotelman cannot follow their lead. True personal service cannot be mechanized or automated, and even though certain mass production techniques are being instituted by hotelmen to relieve them of routine tasks, the human element is the *determining* element of the hospitality business.

Anyone considering an occupational choice naturally tries to discern both the advantages and the disadvantages of the particular vocation he is interested in; like most businesses, hotel management has its own characteristic advantages and disadvantages. There are certain aspects of the profession that are unique. For example, under one roof there may be from five to nine separate, yet coordinated, businesses operating simultaneously. Such a situation guarantees jobs that are challenging as well as diversified. Another factor which promotes interest and provides a challenge is the presence of the human element we have just discussed—the consumer himself. Of course not all positions provide guest contact, but those that do assure the employee association with persons in all walks of life. He will meet and serve the wealthy and the poor, the famous and the notorious, the engaging and the obnoxious, the cooperative and the difficult. Each person who enters a hotel offers the employee an opportunity to learn about human nature and the challenge to provide service that will enhance the guest's stay.

In an age of specialization and mechanization, where pride in workmanship and the satisfaction of carrying through a job from start to finish are nearly extinct, the hotel industry offers the worker not only the responsibility for his product but also the added satisfaction of witnessing the customer's satisfaction and of personally receiving his approval. From the standpoint of working conditions, a hotel offers a clean, safe, pleasant environment. From the standpoint of advancement, hotel managers and department heads traditionally have worked their way up through the ranks; the industry is one which lends itself to academic training, but one in which there is no substitute for experience.

Hotelkeeping is a variable industry that quickly reflects any changes in the national economy. It is a type of business in which techniques, ideas, and modes of operation undergo continual alteration. For a hotel to remain static is actually for it to deteriorate—the famous Ritz in New York is a case in point. One of the famous hostelries of its time, the Ritz had become a landmark and a hallmark of service, yet, because it did not keep up with the times, forty years after its opening it was obsolete and had to be torn down.

Cooperation Essential

Mention was made earlier of the necessity for cooperation and coordination among the various hotel departments. Practically every service offered guests requires the efforts of two or more departments. As an example, to get an incoming guest from the lobby to his freshly cleaned room involves the front office, the uniformed services, and the housekeeping department. Whether it be the serving of a single meal in the coffee shop or the handling of a large convention, the joint efforts of several departments must be coordinated to assure successful and satisfactory service to the customer. Failure on the part of any one department or any one person in that department means unsatisfactory service and a dissatisfied guest. This necessity for individual and departmental cooperation emphasizes even more the inevitabilty of recognizing the human element, not only from the standpoint of the consumer, but also from the standpoint of the employee. No other industry demands such a degree of mutual endeavor.

Rarely does an employee who sells or serves a product have any control over its preparation, production, or quality (an exception is the small hotel where there is limited departmentalization and where everyone from the manager on down must be a Jack-of-all-trades). This aspect of the business can be illustrated by several examples).

1. The hotel sales representative sells a Mr. Johnson—a local businessman—the "Mark Twain Room" for a sales meeting, and arranges for a luncheon in the "Gold Room" and an evening banquet in the ballroom. The sales representative makes the arrangements, but the actual setup of the rooms, the preparation and service of the meals, and the general decorative arrangements are handled by departments over which the sales representative has no control. Should anything prove unsatisfactory, however, Mr. Johnson would hold the sales representative directly responsible.

2. A Mr. and Mrs. Samuels approach the front desk. The room clerk sells them suite 1403 and strongly recommends the "Grill Room" for dinner and dancing. The clerk has no control over the cleanliness and orderliness of the suite or of the food and service in the Grill Room, but the Samuels' satisfaction or lack of it will be transmitted to him.

3. A patron in the coffee shop orders his dinner from the waitress. Service is a bit slow due to a slight accident in the kitchen, and the steak is a little too well done to suit the customer. He makes his displeasure known to the waitress and

blames her, never considering the possibility that she did not contribute to or could not in any way alleviate the situation.

There can be no doubt that situations such as these create tension and increase the possibility of emotional flare-ups among the employees and between employees and guests. But at the same time, many employees feel that this aspect of the hotel business also creates interest because it represents a challenge that cannot be found in any comparable job. These examples should further emphasize the need for careful selection and continuous training of employees.

Qualifications

The majority of hourly paid jobs in a hotel are of a semiskilled nature, and the average person desiring such positions can readily learn the motor skills and regular routines that are called for. Whether or not these persons possess the correct mental and emotional makeup is another question. I have interviewed hundreds of candidates for hotel employment; when asked why they considered themselves good prospects for hotel work, 90 percent of them answered, "I like people," evidently believing this to be the principal qualification for success in the industry. To like people is necessary, but by itself it is not enough. You must be able to adjust rapidly to a variety of unexpected and unpredictable situations and to control your emotions even when under tremendous pressure to defend yourself or speak up for what you know is right. As you move upward in the management hierarchy, you must display leadership and persuasive and analytical qualities that will gain you the cooperation and respect of your subordinates. The higher positions demand special technical know-how, but the principal trait necessary at this level is the ability, through cooperation, to get employees to do what you want done in the way you want it done, and when you want it done.

A final highly desirable characteristic is wholehearted interest and dedication to the hotel business. All leaders possess this quality, and so do the best hotel employees with long service records.

The hotel industry is a twenty-four hour day, seven-day week business. As such, it means that employees are often required to work while other people are relaxing or enjoying a holiday. Because it is a service industry, personal contact is frequent and the employee must sometimes accept abuse from a guest for a situation (which may be real or imaginary) over which the employee has no control. The general wage scale of hotels is lower than that of the manufacturing trades and some other industries. The past ten years have seen a substantial increase in wages. In addition, hotels now come under the federal wage and hour laws. There is little doubt that hotel positions will soon be competitive with comparable jobs in other industries.

Hotel work by nature is characterized by peaks and valleys in business volume, and as a result, a certain degree of tension pervades the atmosphere. Therefore one who cannot easily adjust to busy and quiet cycles of work should not enter most phases of hotel operation. The occupational hazards of the hotel executive are reputed to be ulcers, high blood pressure, and coronary thrombosis; although said in jest, there is some truth in this. As in most industries, hotel positions rank from high to low on the social prestige scale, but it is conceded that, in general, a career in the hotel industry enjoys the highest prestige of any of the occupations in the service industry field.

All in all, viewing both the desirables and the drawbacks, it is my opinion that the advantages of a career in hotel management far outweigh the disadvantages. Once hotel work really gets into your blood, you won't trade professions for any amount of money. This love for the business comes only with experience, but it typifies the genuine hotelman. Ellsworth Milton Statler, the greatest hotelman of all time, lived by his motto, "Life is service."

Part Two

The Organization of
Hotel Operations

CHAPTER 3

The Front of the House

INTRODUCTION

The model hotel organization plan does not exist. The plan for a particular hotel evolves from the influence of a number of factors, principal among which are the location, the type of service offered, the structural layout of the hotel, the background and training of the manager, the personality and abilities of the entire management group, and the type of ownership. Despite such varied differences the three typical organizational plans presented in this chapter will be helpful in gaining a concept of overall hotel operation.

Regardless of how they may be departmentalized, all hotels perform the same basic functions. The chapter and the succeeding chapters of Part Two are devoted to an explanation of the functions performed by each department and the role played by each position within a department. These chapters are designed to give you a good grasp of the variety of duties performed and of the importance of these duties to hotel operation as a whole. To instruct you on *how* to perform a certain job is beyond the scope of this book; the list of suggested readings in the appendix is provided as a guide to factual up-to-date information of a technical nature.

In hotel parlance, a person works either in the "front of the house" or the "back of the house." These two terms are in wide usage and will probably continue to be for years to come. Recently, however, there has been a movement to eliminate the latter term and substitute "catering department." The reasoning for this change is that back of the house could be taken as implying a position of secondary status and importance. Catering department, on the other hand, is more indicative of equal rank and stature. I prefer the later terminology, and have used it throughout this book.

Front-of-the-house operations embody a variety of departments whose functions are integrated primarily for the purpose of rooming guests in the most courteous and satisfactory manner possible. The usual front-of-the-house departments are the Front Office, the Uniformed Service, and the Housekeeping Department; the Engineering Department operates in all areas of the hotel, but it will be discussed in this chapter. Personnel, Accounting, and Sales are specialized departments of a semi-staff nature and they are discussed in Chapters 5 and 6. While the functions performed in different hotels are basically the same, specific methods, procedures, and forms vary from hotel to hotel. For the examples and discussions in this chapter I have assumed a typical 300-room first-class hotel.

THE FRONT OFFICE

The importance of the front office cannot be overemphasized. It is the nerve center, the contact point—it is the liaison between guest and hotel. Often it is said that to the guest the front office is the hotel. The well-known hotelman Mr. Charles O'Toole pictures the hotel as a wheel, of which the front office is the hub. This department is the first that is contacted by an arriving guest, it is the information center during his stay, and it is the last point contacted when he leaves. If a guest begins his stay in a pleasant frame of mind, because of front office courtesy and service, the chances are excellent that he will be favorably disposed toward the other hotel services; but let the front office err, delay, or be indifferent, and the effects will be felt throughout the hotel.

Functions and Supervision

The basic functions of the front office are (1) to process reservations and all communications with persons seeking the hotel's accommodations, (2) to register guests and assign rooms, (3) to handle all mail, telegrams, and messages for guests, (4) to provide financial and credit accommodations, and (5) to furnish information about the hotel, the community, and any special attractions or events of interest.

Supervisory responsibility for these functions will vary in different hotels, but their nature and the mechanics of performing them are common to all front offices. An inspection of Figures 1, 2, and 3—organization charts for a large, a medium, and a small hotel—will give you an idea of the typical areas of front office supervision.

Operation

To illustrate front office operation, we will discuss the procedure that is used by a first-class, medium-sized hotel such as that

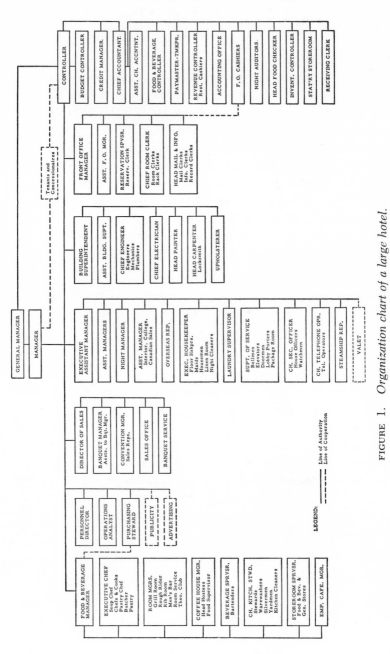

FIGURE 1.   Organization chart of a large hotel.

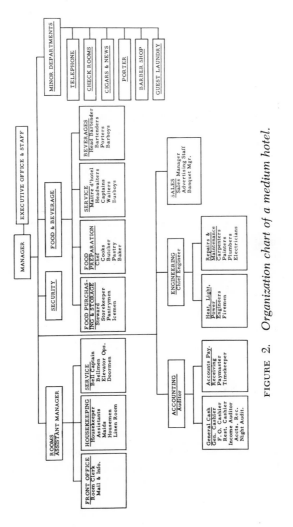

FIGURE 2. *Organization chart of a medium hotel.*

portrayed by Figure 2; for easier comprehension, we will follow it in chronological order.

Arrival of Reservations. Reservation requests arrive by telephone, telegraph, teletype, or across the desk. They are channeled immediately to the office of the assistant to the general manager, where clerks index them, check the guest history file, and make appropriate notations on the correspondence itself. (Practices vary, but usually the guest history file contains information on every guest who has visited the hotel during the past five years.) The majority of routine requests are handled by the office personnel, but conventions are referred directly to the assistant to the general manager for personal attention.

Control Sheet. Correspondence is then sent to the reservation clerk, whose first step is to enter the reservation on the control sheet (Figure 4), noting the type of room desired and the checkout date. (The control number assigned will appear on all records from this point until the guest arrives. Also, you will notice that on the lower portion of the control sheet the suites and special accommodations are treated separately.) With the control number assigned, the clerk now completes the reservation sheet—Figure 5. Each space is filled in, and the control number is noted in the box in the right-hand corner as illustrated. The reservation sheet is then filed alphabetically in the reservation folder for the date of the guest's arrival. As shown by Figures 4 and 5, a Mr. and Mrs. John Antonelli desire a twin-bed room at the minimum rate for three days beginning May 3. They plan to arrive by 9 P.M., reservations were made by letter, the control number is 122, and the reservation has been guaranteed by the Continental Oil Company. Having filed the reservation sheet, the clerk fills out the "yellow sheet" (Figure 6), stamps the correspondence with the information in the box titled "Booked," attaches the yellow sheet to the correspondence, and returns the correspondence to the secretary for answering and filing. All let-

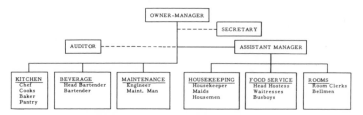

FIGURE 3. *Organization chart of a small hotel.*

ters of confirmation contain the date, the type of accommodation, the number of days requested, and the control number. When a reservation request fails to mention the length of stay the hotel confirms the reservation for one day only. If the prospective guest plans to stay longer he should immediately so notify the hotel, and the reservation will be set up on the basis of the new and complete information. Hotels never confirm specific rooms and usually quote a rate range rather than a set figure.

Reservation Chart. In the reservation office the clerk sets up reservation charts (see Figure 7) for each month, and every reservation is blocked on this chart as soon as it is booked. These charts may be set up as far in advance as the hotel desires. A quick glance at this chart informs the clerk whether or not he can fill a particular reservation request.

Overbooking. Up to this point you could easily gain the impression that handling hotel reservations is a rather simple mechanical and routine job; however, it is not quite as simple as it might appear. The ideal situation, of course, is to have every room booked and every reservation honored. Naturally no hotel can hope to have all of its rooms filled every night of the year, but when the business is available, it is, to say the least, uneconomical to have one or more rooms vacant. As Cornell's Dean Meek so aptly phrased it, "There is no commodity more perishable

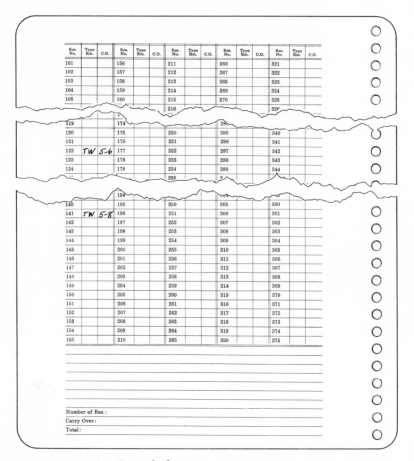

FIGURE 4. *Control Sheet*

than a hotel room. If it is not sold tonight, it can never be sold."
But how does a hotel protect itself against last-minute cancellations and "no-shows?" The answer is by overbooking according to rather reliable estimates, previous records, and guesses—a little crystal-ball gazing might be helpful too. Experience tells us that we can expect about 5 percent no-shows and from 8 to 10 percent cancellations. As a result, the house will be overbooked by this

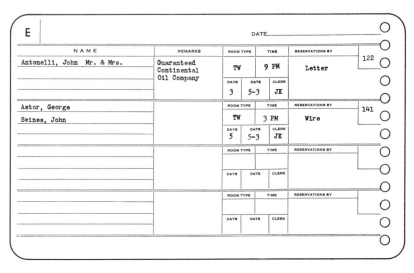

E			DATE___					
NAME	**REMARKS**	**ROOM TYPE**		**TIME**	**RESERVATIONS BY**		122	
Antonelli, John Mr. & Mrs.	Guaranteed Continental Oil Company	TW		9 PM	Letter			
		DAYS	**DATE**	**CLERK**				
		3	5-3	JK				
Astor, George		**ROOM TYPE**		**TIME**	**RESERVATIONS BY**		141	
Seines, John		TW		3 PM	Wire			
		DAYS	**DATE**	**CLERK**				
		5	5-3	JK				
		ROOM TYPE		**TIME**	**RESERVATIONS BY**			
		DAYS	**DATE**	**CLERK**				
		ROOM TYPE		**TIME**	**RESERVATIONS BY**			
		DAYS	**DATE**	**CLERK**				

FIGURE 5.   *Reservation sheet.*

amount less 5 percent, which has been found to be typical carry-over. If these percentages were always wholly accurate the practice of overbooking would never boomerang. But, as in the majority of such operations, there are times when things go awry: no one cancels, or all reservations are honored, or a heavy snow grounds all outgoing planes and carry-over requests are tripled. These are just a few of the incidents that can create a full house and the situation of thirty people waving reservation confirmations under the room clerk's nose and demanding rooms that just aren't available. At such times room clerks can do their courteous best to explain the circumstances and to help find the guests good accommodations elsewhere, but in the majority of cases the guest understands only that he has a confirmed reservation and there is no room for him. Needless to say, such situations can easily lose customers for a hotel. Overbooking is a gamble, but one that must be taken if the hotel is going to produce the revenue expected by the owners. You should realize that rarely does the gamble boomerang.

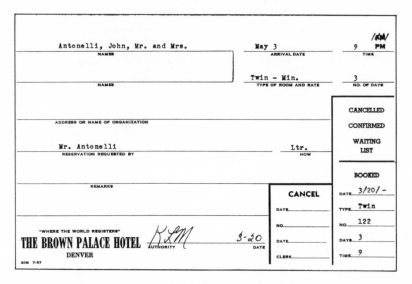

FIGURE 6. *Reservation "yellow sheet."*
(Courtesy Brown Palace Hotel.)

Blocking. Once the reservation has been blocked on the reservation chart and confirmed, no further action is necessary until about a week or ten days before the guest arrives. At this time all reserved rooms are blocked in the room rack in the front office. Any of several kinds of cards, or "blocks," may be used, depending upon the hotel policies and the type of rack. In our example hotel we find three types, identical except for color. A blue block is used for the type of room of which the hotel has many; the room clerk, in attempting to assign a new guest a room, knows that blue blocks can be easily moved around in the rack. An orange block can be moved only if the clerk can find other accommodations of the exact same nature. A yellow block cannot be moved for any reason; yellow blocks are used for suites and accommodations set aside for important guests. While the room clerk has the privilege of shifting rack blocks in order to sell all available rooms, he is also responsible for seeing that all

Room			1	2	3	4	5	6	7	8	9	10			May 19—									29	30
															11	12	13	14	15	16	17	18			
602				Johnson											James										
603			Boles		Gase																				
604				Drake																					
605				Gregory																					
606			Conodo			Jolson																			
607						Rice																			
608						Ross																			
609					Earl																				
610																									
611																									
612																									
613																									
614																									
615																									
616																									
617																									
618																									
619																									
620																									

FIGURE 7. *Reservation chart.*

confirmed reservations are honored. Once the rack is blocked, the reservation procedure is concluded, except in the case of cancellations, which follow the same path as reservation requests.

Room Clerk. Each morning the reservation file for that day is sent to the room clerk in the front office. When the day room clerk reports for duty he receives a report from the night room clerk, looks over the front office log, and receives the reservation count made by the night clerk during his shift. The night clerk has inspected the rack and counted the number of checkouts for the day and to this total added the number of vacant rooms. By subtracting the number of reservations for the day he knows how many rooms are available for sale across the desk or how many rooms the hotel is short. As an example, for a certain day the night clerk counts 69 expected checkouts and 3 vacant rooms. Reservations for that day total 96. His report shows 69 plus 3 minus 96, equals minus 24, and the day clerk knows that 24 rooms must be picked up during the day in order to satisfy all expected customers. Unless there are unexpected checkouts or

FIGURE 8. *Housekeeper's report. (Courtesy Brown Palace Hotel.)*

"WHERE THE WORLD REGISTERS"

The Brown Palace Hotel
Denver, Colorado

Housekeeper's Report

Time 8⁴⁵ AM   5-2 19

Remarks

200s	300s	400s	500s	600s	700s	800s	900s
(200)	300X	400	500	600	700	805	901
(202)	302	402	502	602	702	807	902
204	304	404	504	604	704	809	903
201	301	401	501	601	701	811	904
203	303	403	503	603	.703	812	905
205	305	405	505	605	705	815	906
207	307	407	507	607	707	819	907
209	309	409	509	609	709	825	908
211	311	411	511	611	(711)	827	909
213	313	413	513	613	713	831	910
215	315	415	515	615	715	833	911
217	317	417	517	617	717	835	912
225	319	419	519	619	719	837	914
227	321	421	521	621	721	838	915
229	327	423	523B	623	723	839	916
231	329	427	527	627	725	840	917
233	331	429	529	629	727	841	918
235	333	431	531	631	729	842	919
237	335	433	533	633	731	843	920
239	337	435	535	635	733	844	921
241	339	437	537	637	735	845	922
243	341	439	539	639	737	846	923
206	343	441	541	641	739	847	924
208	306	443	543	643	741	848	925
210	308	406	506	606	743	849	926
212	310	408	508	608	706	850	
214	312	410	510	610	708	852	
228	314	412	512	612	710	853	
230	316	414	514	614	712		
232	318	416	516	616	714		
234	320	418	518	618	716		
238	322	420	520	620	718		
240	324	422	522	622	720		
	326	424	524	624	722		
	328	426	526	626	724		
	330	428	528	628	726		
	332	430	530	630	728		
	334	432	532	632	730		
	336	434	534	634	734		
	338	436	536	636	738		
	340	438	538	638	740		
		440	540	640			

Rooms occupied without baggage

Rooms with baggage not occupied

Occupied-
Out of order-Circle
Occupied without baggage-X

Sleep out B
Vacant Rooms in order-no mark

cancellations the clerk will not be able to sell any rooms to people approaching the desk without reservations.

Housekeeper's Report. Within the first two hours of the day shift, the housekeeper's report (Figure 8) comes to the front office. The room clerk carefully checks the information on the report against the room rack. Any discrepancy between the two is reported to the executive assistant manager and investigated immediately. As an example, the housekeeper's report might list two rooms as being vacant (rooms 731 and 733 in Figure 8), but the rack might show them as being occupied. A quick check would tell that these two rooms are *guaranteed* reservations which are always carried as occupied because the hotel will be paid whether the space is used or not. Sleep-outs (persons registered in the hotel who do not sleep in their rooms on a given night) with or without baggage and rooms occupied without baggage are always checked, since most hotels still face the problem of a certain percentage of skippers—people who fail to check out and pay their bill before leaving the hotel.

Registration, Room Slips. His rack in order and checked, the room clerk is now ready to handle arriving guests, answer inquiries and complaints, and take care of any details listed in the log. His principal job during the day will be rooming guests —a procedure fairly simple but vitally important. Returning to our illustrative guests, Mr. and Mrs. Antonelli approach the desk where they are greeted by the room clerk, who inquires whether they have a reservation. Having made a reservation, Mr. Antonelli gives the clerk his confirmation. While Mr. Antonelli is filling out the registration card the room clerk checks the reservation sheet, notes the arrival, and from the rack picks out the room number blocked for Mr. and Mrs. Antonelli. Returning to the desk he records the room number and rate on the registration card and checks to see that all the necessary information has been provided; he then fills out (in duplicate) the room slip

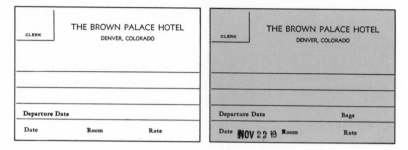

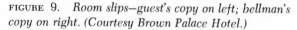

FIGURE 9. *Room slips—guest's copy on left; bellman's copy on right. (Courtesy Brown Palace Hotel.)*

shown in Figure 9. He signals the front bellman, hands him the key and slips, and courteously wishes the Antonellis a pleasant stay.

The room slip serves several purposes. One copy goes to the guest for verifying the correct spelling of his name, the room number and rate, and the checkout date. The other copy goes to the bellman, who notes the presence or absence of baggage and whether or not it is light, and then returns the slip to the desk. If there is no baggage, the guest, unless he is known to the hotel, will be asked for payment in advance.

As soon as the guest leaves the desk, the clerk routes the registration card to the girl filling the dual role of information clerk and typist. She types an information card in triplicate and an accounting folio in duplicate, each listing the name and address of the guest, the room number and rate, and the checkout date. The information cards go to the room rack, the information rack, and the telephone-department rack; the accounting folio goes to the front office cashier. The registration card is then filed, as required by law. The procedure for selling a room that has not been reserved is the same as that just described. One minor exception is that the room clerk will place a tab in the rack space of the assigned room, which will remain there until the information card returns from the typist. This is simply to prevent the clerk from selling the same room to two different people during a busy checkin period.

Once the guest is roomed, his chief contact with the front office will be through the mail and information clerk—a one-person position in medium-sized hotels. In some hotels the room clerk may also handle mail, messages, information, and keys. In large metropolitan hotels there is a higher degree of specialization, and often there may be room clerks, mail clerks, information clerks, and key clerks. Regardless of the number of positions, the important point is that the guest receive all of these services quickly and properly.

Telephone Department. A department that the guest will never see but one with which he may have frequent contact is the telephone department. Presided over by a chief operator, who may or may not occupy a switchboard position, this group handles all intra-hotel, local, and long-distance calls. Since there are charges for telephone service, an operator must log all calls and see to it that the charges are sent to the front office cashier for posting to the proper guest accounts. Although an operator never sees the guests, her voice and telephone manner can influence either favorably or unfavorably a guest's opinion of the hotel and its service. Another essential function of this department is awakening, at the correct time, those guests who have left calls. A recent court case in New York emphasizes the importance of performing this function properly: a guest sued a well-known hotel for $200,000 because, due to an operator's negligence, he was not awakened and consequently lost a business transaction.

Guest's Account—Departure. During his stay at the hotel, the average guest charges several items to his account. Mr. and Mrs. Antonelli, for example, might have had several items of clothing cleaned and pressed and also might have sent clothing to the laundry. Perhaps Mr. Antonelli made a series of long-distance calls. And the couple may have eaten their meals in the hotel, with Mr. Antonelli signing the checks. All of these charges would be sent by the individual departments concerned to the front office cashier, whose responsibility it is to see to their posting to the Antonelli account folio. Accuracy is mandatory in this position, for an error resulting in either overcharging or undercharging would harm the hotel. It is true that the cashier's records are checked daily by the night auditor, but many times the check comes too late to counteract an error.

On May 6, in our example, Mr. Antonelli goes to the cashier's window and notifies her that room 632 is checking out. She quickly totals all charges on Mr. Antonelli's folio and presents him with his bill. Payment is recorded, and the Antonellis leave the hotel. Since she usually is the hotel's last contact with guests, the cashier has the opportunity to send them on their way in a happy frame of mind.

Although the guest has departed, the front office procedure is not yet complete. The cashier notifies the room clerk that room 632 has checked out. He folds over the information card, but leaves it in the rack. A folded-over card indicates that the guest has checked out but that the room has not been reported in order by the housekeeper. The information clerk, housekeeper, and chief operator are also notified of the checkout. As soon as the housekeeper reports the room in order the information card will be removed from the rack. Indicating a room vacant but not in order lets the room clerk sell it, but usually he will not permit a new guest to occupy the room until it is in order. To allow a guest to enter a disorderly room is almost surely to result in his gaining a bad impression. Most hotels will allow a guest to enter a disorderly room if he insists, but there are still a few that stand strictly by their policy that no guest shall ever be roomed until his accommodations are in order.

Night Clerk. The night clerk, working the 11-7 graveyard shift, usually does little rooming of guests, although he does handle any late arrivals entering the hotel during his tour of duty. The first task of the night clerk is making out his revenue report as soon as possible after he comes on duty; using a regular form listing all the rooms in the hotel, he notes the occupancy and revenue for each room, taking his information from the room rack. This report details the room revenue for the hotel each day. The night clerk compares his report with the night auditor's figures, and the two must agree. Any discrepancies are checked and rechecked until the error is found and agreement is reached. As mentioned earlier, the night clerk makes a reservation count before going off duty and passes this information on to the day clerk. He also records in the log any unusual or important happenings and handles any inquiries. During most of his shift the night clerk is in charge of the hotel, since the night manager usually leaves by midnight. However, the manager lives in, so should anything of a serious nature arise during the night the night clerk knows that he can be reached immediately. Either the manager or his assistant are always available to handle unexpected or emergency situations.

SECURITY

Fulfilling a vitally important function behind the scenes in every hotel is the security officer, or house detective as he is often called. He has the dual responsibility of protecting both the guest and the hotel from harm. Hotels and their guests are vulnerable targets for prowlers, thieves, confidence men, and other undesirables. Consequently, the security officer and his staff of watchmen must be vigilant every hour of the day. For obvious reasons, hotels prefer not to have the methods and techniques of their security force publicized, but the types of problems can be discussed briefly.

The most persistent problem the security department must deal with is the combined one of doors being left unlocked or keys being left in the outside lock. Reliable statistics indicate that every night from 10 percent to 20 percent of the doors in a hotel will be left unlocked. Nothing could be more inviting to the prowler or thief intent on victimizing the hotel and its guests. Another problem faced by hotels is the choice of their establishments by confidence men as a base for operations. The security officer must spot such persons as rapidly as he can and, if legally possible, get them out of the hotel.

Every security officer has experienced the problem of the guest who cannot be satisfied and who is continually finding fault. He is the type who antagonizes every employee who serves him and generally has the house in an uproar. Because he is completely obnoxious he is asked to leave but, bombarding everybody with insults, he refuses. Everyone having reached the limit of their patience, he is forcibly ejected. Then within a day the hotel is sued, and the obnoxious guest wins a nice cash settlement—which is exactly what he was seeking. This country has a goodly number of crooked persons living very comfortably off the income from suits against hotels where the security officer or a member of the management team lost his temper and played right into their hands.

One of the hotel world's most feared danger is fire. Modern hotels have every feature of fireproof construction and every fire prevention technique known; however, some older hotels, especially frame-constructed resorts, are faced with tremendous fire prevention problems. Regardless of how fireproof the building, this danger is ever present, the guest himself being the biggest cause of fires. Although he knows better, a guest will smoke in bed, or he will drink too much and become careless with cigarettes and matches. The security force must be always alert for any potential hazard or any indication of fire. Members of the force are even encouraged not to smoke so that they will be better able to detect fire.

There is always the problem of inebriates. Handling someone who is intoxicated is never easy, but when the person is a hotel guest the situation becomes *very* delicate. Just as there are all stages of drunkenness, there are all types of drunken persons, and each must be handled differently. The security officer must reason, plead, cajole, and if necessary use his power of arrest, to keep such individuals from disturbing other guests or possibly harming themselves. Cutting off a guest's room service is usually the first step.

Another situation that must be handled with extreme caution is the investigation of people in a room who may be there illegally. One false move or an unwarranted accusation by the security officer may prove harmful to the hotel. Still, he must be forceful and efficient in removing individuals who have no right to be in a room.

All accidents, especially those in which the hotel may be liable, have to be investigated and followed through and the security officer must write a detailed report of the case. Unless the security officer is diligent in this duty a hotel can easily be paying accident claims for which it has no responsibility. Lest you gain the impression that accidents are investigated purely for monetary reasons, rest assured that any reputable hotel is vitally interested in the welfare of its guests and will often go to extra expense to see that the guest receives even special services.

What type of individual makes a good security officer? Although special police training is not deemed mandatory, the majority of hotel security officers do have law enforcement backgrounds, they must know in detail all local and state laws pertaining to hotels, and they must actively cooperate with police authorities. An even temperament, an alert mind, and a high standard of personal values and ethics are other desirable prerequisites of a security officer, many times a year he will have to refuse bribes, gifts, and favors offered him to overlook certain activities taking place in a hotel. He must be able to gain the cooperation of people—both guests and employees—and his success depends on this ability more than on any other single trait. But every manager must remember that a security officer is only as good as the backing he receives from the management.

THE UNIFORMED SERVICE

This department is aptly named because its only product is service. The workers of this department perform their duties before the eyes of the guest and have more guest contact than any other department. None of the jobs are complex, but their functions are important, since members of the uniformed service are the first to greet and the last to contact the hotel guest.

The uniformed service comprises the doorman, bellmen, elevator starters, and elevator operators. Lobby porters may be included in this department, but they are often a part of the housekeeping department. In large hotels a superintendent of service, who may have an assistant, directs the uniformed service. In small hotels the two head bellmen supervise this department but are under the jurisdiction of either the assistant to the manager or the executive assistant manager.

The doorman is the hotel's greeter. Stationed at the main lobby entrance he meets all arriving guests and helps to unload luggage. He guards the luggage of arriving and departing guests and helps the bellman in baggage handling. He summons taxis for patrons and usually supervises the parking of guest cars. The doorman should be well informed on points of interest and locations of buildings because he will often be asked for such information.

The bellman's principal duty is rooming guests. As mentioned in a previous section, the front bellman is called to the desk to receive the room slips and the key. He sees if the guest has any mail or messages, carries the baggage, and escorts the guest to the elevator and to his room. A good bellman will check the room for orderliness and proper functioning of lights, explain services to the guest, answer any questions, and leave the key in the inside door lock. His courtesy, tact, and efficiency can solidify the feeling of welcome already generated by the room clerk. In their frequent trips to all parts of the hotel, bellmen are the eyes and ears of the hotel; it is their duty to report anything out of the ordinary. Other duties include assisting the departing guest with his luggage, running errands and handling messages, paging guests, and carrying baggage on room changes. At various times bellmen are called upon to show rooms to patrons or to conduct group tours through the hotel.

Elevator starters supervise the elevator operators, regulate elevator speed and flow, and inspect elevators for cleanliness. It is extremely important at times of heavy traffic to have all of the elevators moving efficiently. Guests do not like to wait, and a crowd milling around the elevators does nothing to enhance the hotel's reputation nor does it add to the guests' pleasure. The elevator operator must be courteous at all times and must have all passenger destinations correct. In small hotels there is increasing use of self-service elevators in an attempt to keep payroll costs from rising.

THE HOUSEKEEPING DEPARTMENT

Executive Housekeeper, Linen-Room Supervisor

One of the busiest and most important department heads in a hotel is the executive housekeeper. On her shoulders rests the responsibility for the cleanliness of most of the hotel as well as the neatness and orderliness of the guest rooms. The true scope of housekeeping escapes most casual observers and the majority of hotel guests. To conduct her department the executive house-keeper usually has an assistant and several supervisors—the number depends on the number of rooms in the hotel. Our example hotel has one supervisor for every two floors, or, being an eight-floor building, a total of four. It should be stated that most housekeepers expect their supervisors to work as well as to give orders. Since the department has varied divisions of work, each will be covered individually.

The headquarters of the housekeeping department is the linen room. The office is in the charge of linen room supervisors who work in three shifts, and it is manned twenty-four hours a day. In this office is the telautograph (an electrical communication device similar to the teletype), which connects directly with the front office, the engineer, and the shop. This office also has direct contact by telephone and a light signaling system with the maid's locker on each floor. All orders and requests pertaining to housekeeping pass through the linen room, with the majority of

FIGURE 10. *Housekeeping log. (Courtesy Brown Palace Hotel.)*

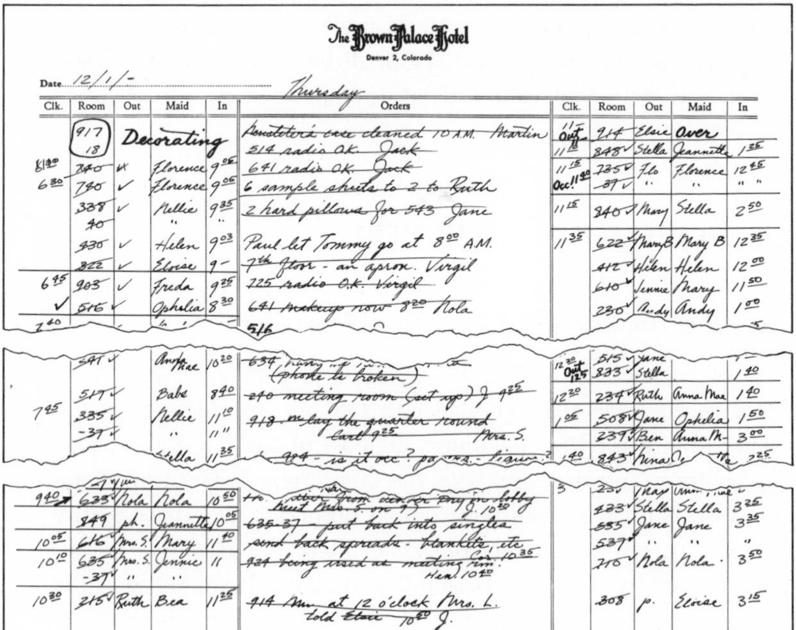

communications being with the front office. Every order is written in the housekeeping log, and when an order is completed a line is drawn through it. Figure 10 shows a portion of the log.

Checkout Procedure

As soon as a guest checks out the room clerk notifies housekeeping, via the telautograph, who enters the room number in their log with a notation of the time the checkout is received. The supervisor calls the checkout to the proper floor and enters in the "Out" column (see Figure 10) the name of the maid or the houseman who receives the call. When the floor reports the room in order the name of the person reporting goes in the "Maid" column and the time goes in the "In" column. In Figure 10 you will notice that all checkouts received before 8 A.M. have only a check mark in the "Out" column. The maids do not go on the floor until 8 A.M., so checkouts prior to that time are marked on a slip which the maids pick up when they go on duty.

As a double check on available rooms the room clerk calls daily to "check the rack," or "page the rack" as the procedure is often called. He gives the room numbers, and the housekeeping office reports whether or not they are in order. To facilitate this

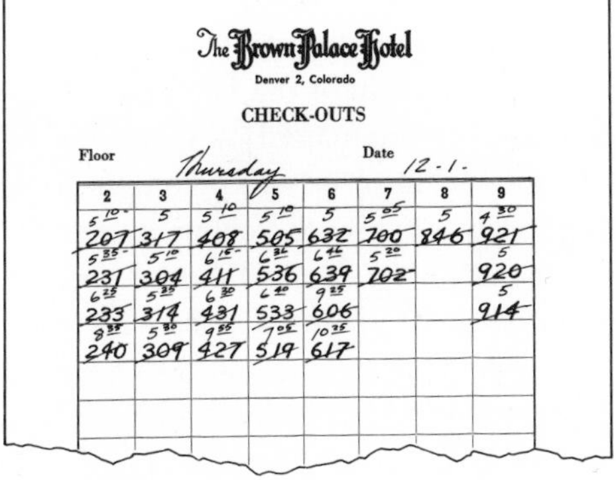

The Brown Palace Hotel
Denver 2, Colorado

CHECK-OUTS

Floor *Thursday* Date *12-1-*

2	3	4	5	6	7	8	9
5^{10} 207	5 317	5^{10} 408	5^{10} 505	5 632	5^{05} 700	5 846	4^{30} 921
5^{35} 231	5^{10} 304	6^{15} 411	6^{32} 536	6^{46} 639	5^{20} 702		5 920
6^{25} 233	5^{35} 314	6^{30} 431	6^{40} 533	9^{25} 606			5 914
8^{35} 240	5^{30} 309	9^{55} 427	7^{05} 519	10^{25} 617			

FIGURE 11. *Check-out sheet. (Courtesy Brown Palace Hotel.)*

procedure, the office usually takes the checkouts from the log and places them on the checkout sheet shown in Figure 11. As a room is reported in order the supervisor crosses out the number and enters the time.

The linen room supervisor on the second shift has the same duties as the morning shift girl. Both of these women have a full crew of maids during their duty hours. The night supervisor, working from 11 to 7, is by herself.

Lost and Found, Baby Sitting

Two other duties handled by the housekeeping office are the lost and found service and the baby sitting service. All articles found in the hotel by employees or by anyone else are sent directly to housekeeping. Accurate records are kept, and the items are held for ninety days. All inquiries about lost items are directed to this office. A lost and found report is shown in Figure 12. Not every hotel provides baby sitting, but with the increased emphasis on attracting family business this service is becoming more common. The baby sitters are usually older women who have been investigated and approved by the hotel.

Laundry, Linens

Not all of the activity in the linen room centers around the office. It takes a good many sheets, pillowcases, towels, tablecloths, and napkins to operate a hotel, and that means a big laundry. A large hotel may have its own laundry, but the majority use commercial laundries. We will leave to the technical experts questions as to which method is cheaper and at what point in volume it pays the hotel to do its own laundry. Suffice it to say, with either method the housekeeping department has its share of work. All dirty linens are sent to the soil counting room, and totals are sent to the housekeeper, who keeps the record in her office. Clean laundry comes directly to the linen room, where it is counted,

The Brown Palace Hotel
Denver, Colorado.

DATE *10-31-*

Lost and Found

Room	Date	Hour	Articles	By Whom	Remarks
Lobby	10/30	55	Gold tie clasp	—	In drawer
Phone booth	10/30	55	Woman's black gloves	Guest	" "
Tavern	10/27	55	1 tan hat — fr Baron Size 7⅛	—	In closet
Tavern	10/27	55	1 grey Stetson hat May Co.	—	" "
Lobby	10/29	55	1 tan raincoat Chas. Mac Intosh Eng.	—	" "
310	10/31	55	Ladies red bag containing $90 - car key, etc.	Eloise Ahrens	In office
Hall on 7 Rm 711	10/31	55	Glasses	Frances	Del. by Frances
Rm 414	10/31	55	Bath robe - man (yellow grey)	Helen B.	In drawer
Rm 600	10/31	55	1 box containing (cuff links tie pins, tie clasp, etc.)	Cornelia R.	In drawer

INQUIRY

Room	Date	Hour	Articles	By Whom	Remarks
Ship Tavern	10/30	55	Man's blue topcoat	Called for by Bellman	
838	10/31	55	Sweater	Mr. Meldman	no record
9th flr.	10/28	55	Blue topcoat - keys in pocket - initials J.J.W.	owner will call Miss Corwin 11/1/55	no record
400	10/25	55	P.J. bottoms	returned to owner —	

FIGURE 12. *Lost-and-found report.*
(Courtesy Brown Palace Hotel.)

inspected, and graded to control loss or overcharge, to reveal soiled linen (which will be returned), and to check for tears, rips, or other damage that must be given attention before the piece goes back into service. Linens are graded as "firsts," "seconds," or "third"; thirds are used in the lowest priced rooms, seconds in the average priced rooms, and firsts in the best rooms. Dining room linens are counted, inspected, and then sent to the various rooms on requisition from a dining room captain. Uniforms are checked out to the employees from the linen room. Every evening the maid lockers on each floor are stocked to par with linen in order that the maids will have a ready supply in the morning. The seamstresses who mend the linen work in the linen room. In some hotels, the housekeeping department makes its own draperies and spreads, although the practice is not too common; where it is done, an extra person devotes her time almost exclusively to this function.

Maids and Housemen

The greatest number of employees in the housekeeping department are maids and housemen. For purposes of upgrading, the title "maid" has been changed to "housekeeper" in a number of hotels, but since "maid" is a more common usage I will continue to use it in this chapter. All hotels must employ day maids, but practices vary with regard to night maids. Some hotels, usually the more luxurious types, employ a full staff and provide turn-down service in all rooms; others provide this service only in best rooms, and some do not provide it at all.

To picture the duties of a maid we will follow her on a typical day. Coming on duty she first reports to the housekeeping office where she signs for her keys and picks up the checkout slip showing rooms in her area that have already been vacated. Arriving at her assigned floor she immediately takes a "house count," using a daily report form such as that shown in Figure 13. This report is sent to the housekeeper and provides the data from which she compiles the housekeeper's report (Figure 8), which we discussed under front office operation. Now the maid starts her regular cleaning of rooms, keeping a record of her work on a form such as that shown in Figure 14 (a maid will ordinarily take care of from fourteen to eighteen rooms a day). Before going off

THE BROWN PALACE HOTEL MAID'S DAILY REPORT

Date /-3/- Maid Elsie

Room	Vacant	No Baggage Occupied	Baggage Not Occupied	Occupied	Remarks
907			X		
908			X		
909				X	
910				X	
911				X	
912			X		
914				X	
915				X	

FIGURE 13. *Maid's daily report. (Courtesy Brown Palace Hotel.)*

duty, she takes a clean-linen count. The *night* maid devotes most of her time to turndown service and to providing extra towels, and she attends to any guest needs.

The housemen work in close cooperation with the maids. The usual hotel staffing allots one houseman to every two floors. Regularly the houseman cleans all hallway carpets on his two floors, and at least once a week he cleans the baseboards, Venetian blinds, and carpets of all rooms in his area. Room carpets are swept every day by the maid with her lightweight carpet sweeper, so once-a-week cleaning by the houseman with his heavy sweeper is sufficient to maintain a high degree of cleanliness. Moving furniture to or from guest rooms is the houseman's duty, and he also turns mattresses for the maids.

Maintenance and Redecoration

Regardless of the care given, walls will become soiled, rugs will become stained, and upholstered furniture will periodically require a thorough cleaning. In severe cases of wear, paint will become chipped, furniture will be broken, upholstery will be torn or worn out. To remedy these situations and to keep all rooms in A-1 order is another responsibility of the housekeeping depart-

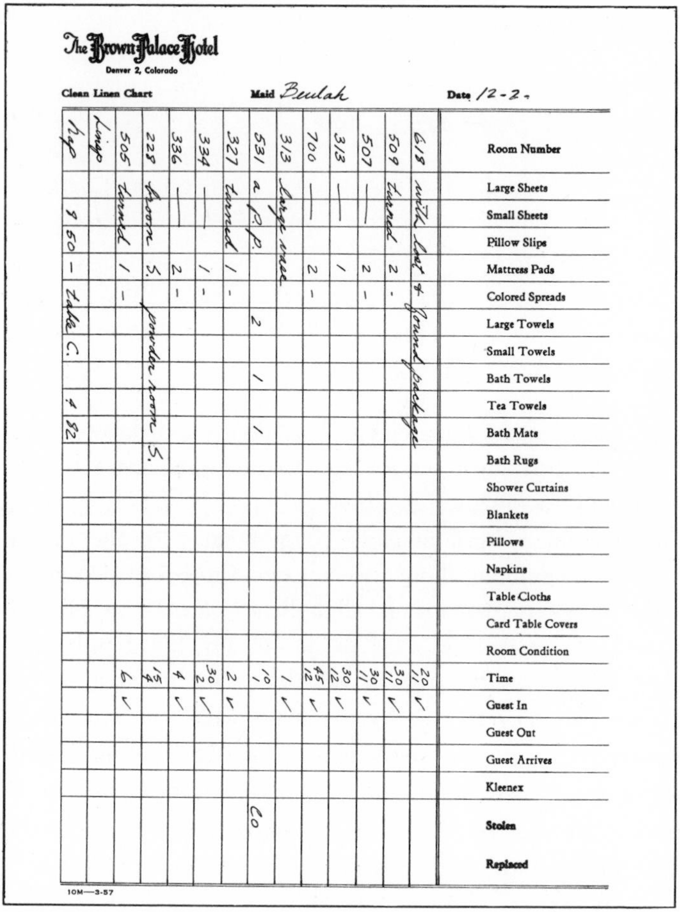

FIGURE 14. *Maid's record. (Courtesy Brown Palace Hotel.)*

ment. Such work is handled by the wallwashers, painters, cabinet makers, upholsterers, and general handymen.

The housekeeper tries to schedule one room every day for wall washing and cleaning. The crew starts on the room in the morning—furniture is moved to the shop where all upholstery is shampooed; the wallwashers clean the walls and shampoo the room carpet—then late in the afternoon, if drying conditions are good, the furniture is returned to the room, and the room may be sold for immediate occupancy. Because out-of-order rooms produce no revenue the housekeeper always strives to keep them to a minimum.

Room redecorating is a more complex undertaking, requiring a room to be out of order for a number of days, since during this time it is stripped completely. Furniture is sent to the shop, where it is repaired, reupholstered, and refinished. The carpet is taken up. The engineer checks and inspects all heating, plumbing, and air conditioning. Only after the room is completely painted and papered are the carpet and furniture moved back. Usually one or two rooms are out of order the year-around for redecorating. When the slack season for the hotel arrives, management generally closes two floors and turns them over to the housekeeper. At this time outside painters are brought in to supplement the regular hotel staff on the redecorating project. Accurate records of all wall washing and redecorating are kept by the housekeeper, and every room will be redecorated completely about every five or six years.

Although the housekeeper concentrates on the guest rooms, her responsibility does not end there. The lobby, all restaurants, public space, and offices must be cleaned, powder rooms have to be kept in order, and rooms for meetings must be set up. To perform these duties, the housekeeping staff includes lobby cleaners, dining room cleaners, night cleaners, powder room maids, and setup men.

As an aid in planning her work, the housekeeper receives a weekly and a daily activity sheet listing all functions or special setups required. In addition to directing those activties we have covered, the housekeeper does all purchasing for the department and plays an active role in interior decorating. One might expect her to have a good deal of guest contact, but such is not the case; usually the only guests the housekeeper sees are those who are ill or those making complaints that pertain to her department.

THE ENGINEERING DEPARTMENT

The engineering department works almost completely behind the scenes but it fulfills a tremendously responsible function. The chief engineer directs the activities of this department and supervises a staff of skilled technicians. The exact titles of engineering positions and the degree of specialization of work by any member of the crew will depend on the size of the hotel and whether or not the department is unionized. Regardless of titles and specialization, the nature of the work is the same in all hotels. The engineering staff of our example hotel includes the chief engineer, five licensed engineers, and five engineers, who are probably best described as general maintenance men; i.e., they perform a variety of duties and are not specifically assigned to any one type of work. Because of long experience, each of these men is skilled in every type of work performed by the department.

The work of the engineering department is divided into six main areas: electrical, plumbing, heating, ventilation and air conditioning, refrigeration, and building maintenance and repair. The hotel's own crew is primarily concerned with maintenance functions in each of these areas, but large installations, changeovers, or new construction are handled by licensed outside contractors. The use of licensed contractors for major jobs is dictated both by city codes and the fact that the engineering crew has insufficient time and manpower to handle such work in addition to attending to regular repair and maintenance.

Electrical Repair

Electrical repair takes the department to every corner of the building. An elaborate electrical system with its many circuits means hundreds of fuses, and every blown fuse must be immediately replaced. Should a fuse continue to burn out, the short circuit must, of course, be located and repaired. All electrical fixtures, outlets, and switches must be kept in good working order. Any extra display lighting, spotlights, movie projectors, or appliances for sales meetings or conventions are handled by engineering. Since a hotel utilizes a tremendous amount of electrical equipment, which must be kept in excellent working order and repaired when necessary, any difficulty of an electrical nature results in an immediate call to the engineering office.

Today the majority of hotels depend upon public service utilities for supplying their electrical power; however, even many of these hotels keep a standby generator ready for immediate use, should the regular source fail. Undoubtedly a few hotels still generate their own power, but to do so requires added staff and equipment and usually results in a cost higher than would be characteristic of public utilities. Maintaining and servicing a *modern* electrical system is involved enough for the engineering department, but consider the woes of an engineer whose hotel may be anywhere from fifty to a hundred years old, and who must contend with equipment and wiring that, by modern standards, is obsolete.

Plumbing

Maintaining the plumbing system of a hotel is no small job. With a complete bathroom for nearly every guest room, and with equipment such as that necessary in a restaurant kitchen, a good-sized hotel has a larger plumbing business than many American communities. In addition to the circulating hot water system, hotels have a separate and complete cold water system—a guest without either hot or cold water wastes no time making his displeasure known, and the engineers are expected to remedy the situation immediately. All modern hotels offer circulating ice water in every room, which is something else to keep the engineering crew busy. Faucet washers are bound to wear out and many hours each week are spent in replacing them. Drains may become stopped by themselves, but when there are dozens or hundreds of guests in a hotel some will inadvertently discard objects, in the washbasin or the bathtub, which will cause drain stoppages. On upper floors plugged drains can be especially damaging if they result in flooding. It is not too uncommon for a maid or a bellman to discover a small river flowing into the hallway from under the door of a guest room. Even a minor flood of this type can be the cause of extensive damage, to say nothing of discomfort to the occupants of the floor immediately below.

Another call frequently received in the engineering office concerns toilets. Whenever this type of call comes in the workman automatically arms himself with the toilet auger and a plunger before proceeding to the room. These two tools are usually sufficient, but in serious cases the toilet may have to be removed to enable the plumber to locate the source of difficulty. Water closet valves must be frequently checked and kept in good working order to avoid noises. A new type of water closet problem has been reported by one hotel engineer, and it serves to point out that engineering problems can originate from the most unpredictable sources. A guest buys a few bottles of beer and takes them to his room for later consumption. Naturally he wants to have his beer cold when he drinks it, so he puts the bottles in the water closet tank. A few hours later the bottles are cold but unknown to him one of the labels has come off. Then the first time the toilet is flushed, shreds of paper clog the valves, and from then on flushing is impossible until the toilet has been removed and taken to the shop for cleaning.

Some of the plumbing work that must be handled by the engineering department can be rather messy and odoriferous. One example is cleaning the kitchen grease traps and the basement grease line. Fortunately the frequency of this job can be decreased by the use of chemicals, but occasionally it still has to be done manually. Adding to the problems of the engineers is the fact that the original plumbing in most hotels probably was not intended for all the usage it now gets. Systems can be modernized gradually, but few establishments can undertake such a job in a short period.

Heating

For a good part of the year the engineer must concern himself with keeping the hotel heated. In the winter this is simply a matter of maintaining a proper, even temperature. During spring and fall, however, it is desirable to take off the chill without overheating the hotel—no small task if the heat is manually controlled. Although hot water heating systems are not uncommon, steam systems are more prevalent, and while many hotels purchase their steam from public utilities, others stoke their own boilers. Buying steam has the advantages of reducing the payroll and of maintaining cleanliness. Coal-stoked boilers are dirty; gas or oil burners are clean, but they still require additional employees. Even those hotels that buy steam must maintain standby boilers, so the engineering crew must have the technical knowledge and skill to handle them. Both the kitchen and the valet service require high-pressure steam, which is usually provided by a separate boiler. To a layman, maintenance of a heating plant may appear to be simple routine work, but in reality it requires varied kinds of highly technical knowledge. Burners must be maintained and repaired, thermostats must be kept in good working order, radiators and valves need attention. It is true that new types of controls are being developed that bring heating closer to an automatic operation, but the robot repair and maintenance man just doesn't exist and probably never will.

Ventilation and Air Conditioning

The next area of maintenance includes ventilation and air conditioning. Regular changes of air are, of course, obligatory, and it takes machinery equipment to provide them. Who assumes responsibility for the proper operation of such equipment? The

engineer and his staff. The public today demands air conditioning in all first-class accommodations. If an engineer is lucky his
hotel will have a central system that is relatively modern, thus
leaving him with a central point for maintenance and repair.
However, if he must take care of a system of individual units,
especially the single-room variety, his work is greatly increased.

Refrigeration

Every hotel requires refrigeration facilities to handle the needs of
the kitchen and the steward's department, and in any hotel large
walk-in boxes, reach-in boxes, and other types of individual units
must operate twenty-four hours a day without interruption. Failure of a reach-in is not too serious if detected reasonably soon,
since the box's contents can be transferred; even if the contents
of a reach-in spoil, it does not involve a major sum of money.
Failure of a filled walk-in, however, would be a different story,
since spoilage here would mean a major loss. Preventing the
possibility of such failures by continual maintenance is the duty of
the engineering department.

General Maintenance and Repair

At such times when it might become necessary to break through
walls in order to carry out plumbing or electrical repairs, the
subsequent wall repair would be taken care of by the engineering
department. The engineers also handle small welding jobs and
the maintenance of door hinges and locks. Major equipment such
as elevators are usually under a maintenance contract for peri-
odic inspection or repair by outside firms. It is obvious that
supervision of the varied work outlined in this section demands
an experienced person possessing broad technical knowledge and
high capabilities. This person must not only conduct his department efficiently, but he must also keep abreast of new develop-

ments, techniques, and equipment in the engineering world. A good engineer makes a great contribution to management peace of mind.

CHAPTER 4

The Catering Department

The word "cater" means to supply. In a hotel the catering department supplies three things: food, beverages, and service. The first two items are tangibles, and with a certain amount of skill and supervision they can be provided to the guest's satisfaction. The third item—service—is an intangible and it requires more than ability or versatility. Skill is, of course, essential in producing good service, but the most important single factor is that the employee who gives the service be pleasant and courteous as well as skillful, for no matter how delicious the food and drink, a guest will not enjoy a meal when service is lacking.

Naturally, persons with varied hotel backgrounds will be reading these words. To the more experienced this outline of the catering department may be too general a picture, perhaps not detailed enough. To the person of little experience it may present a nice overall picture, but one that might give the impression that conducting a profitable food business is a very simple matter. It is to the latter reader that this treatment is principally aimed, and it is to the latter reader that I would offer a word of warning: Every year many people fail in the restaurant business not only because they usually know too little, from a commercial stand-point, about the industry, but also because they hold to this very misconception that the restaurant business is a simple business. Certainly fortunes have been made in the restaurant industry, but they have been made by persons who know that good food and good service are prime requisities, and who from the begin-ning understand that an overall picture, plus a view of the details, means the difference between profit and loss.

Conducting a successful catering operation may seem a relatively easy undertaking: good food plus good service plus the right price equals success! For an abbreviated answer this is the right formula. But because catering is more than just a formula it is necessary, if you would achieve a thorough understanding, to consider some of the problems and some of the people involved in attaining the end result—serving a guest a meal.

Now let us turn to good food, good service, and success!

The catering department of any hotel represents a complex group in which there are many lines of authority and various overlapping functions. The majority of people in this department are never seen by the guest, and few guests are even aware of the numerous persons who have a part in the preparation—direct and indirect—of the meal that is served to them.

The organization chart shown in Figure 15 is the one used by our example hotel, which handles an average monthly food volume of $165,000 and an average monthly beverage volume of $75,000, and it will be referred to in our discussion of the catering department. Although no two hotels are exactly alike, and although all hotels differ in regard to arrangement of author-

FIGURE 15.   *Organization chart—catering department.*

ity and duties of personnel, the points of this discussion will be common to all catering departments. In reference to this organization chart, we will not start at the top and work down, but rather we will begin with the purchasing of raw commodities and follow the various steps until we reach the finished product—the prepared meal served to the guest.

THE FOOD FUNCTION

Purchasing and Receiving

You will observe from the organization chart that the purchasing and the receiving of food are done by the same person, who, of course, is assisted by other people. No doubt you will wonder if it is good business to have one person handle both purchasing and receiving. Normally the answer would be no, but with the type of arrangement shown for our example hotel there are many checks and re-checks which will eliminate or control the problems that would ordinarily be present when one person is responsible for both jobs.

Purchasing. In the food division of the catering department the person who initiates operations is the purchasing steward. He is the first to arrive in the morning, since most of his work is done before the actual preparation of food begins, and each day he must follow a set routine because it is essential that all food be purchased as close as possible to the time it will be used in order to ensure freshness and top quality.

On arriving, the purchasing steward first takes an inventory of the produce and dairy products—items that are purchased every day. Next he checks the banquet menus and the daily menus, as well as the forecast of the number of covers, or guests, to be served that day, and arrives at the amounts and kinds of food to be purchased. These he lists on the form shown in Figure 16, the steward's market quotation list. Note that items normally purchased daily are pre-printed on this sheet; blank spaces are provided so that special items can be written in. The steward lists

FIGURE 16. *Steward's market quotation list.*

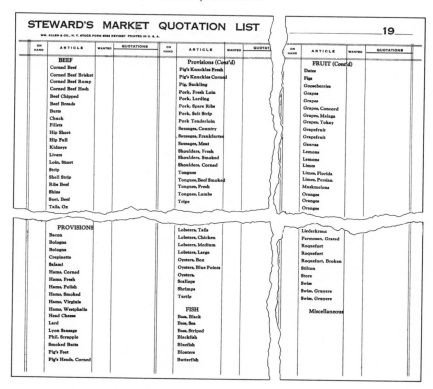

STEWARD'S MARKET QUOTATION LIST

WM. ALLEN & CO., N. Y. STOCK FORM 6085 REVISED PRINTED IN U. S. A.

_____19___

ON HAND	ARTICLE	WANTED	QUOTATIONS	ON HAND	ARTICLE	WANTED	QUOTAT	ON HAND	ARTICLE	WANTED	QUOTATIONS
	BEEF				**Provisions (Cont'd)**				**FRUIT (Cont'd)**		
	Corned Beef				Pig's Knuckles Fresh				Dates		
	Corned Beef Brisket				Pig's Knuckles Corned				Figs		
	Corned Beef Rump				Pig, Suckling				Gooseberries		
	Corned Beef Hash				Pork, Fresh Loin				Grapes		
	Beef Chipped				Pork, Larding				Grapes		
	Beef Breads				Pork, Spare Ribs				Grapes, Concord		
	Butts				Pork, Salt Strip				Grapes, Malaga		
	Chuck				Pork Tenderloin				Grapes, Tokay		
	Fillets				Sausages, Country				Grapefruit		
	Hip Short				Sausages, Frankfurter				Grapefruit		
	Hip Full				Sausages, Meat				Guavas		
	Kidneys				Shoulders, Fresh				Lemons		
	Livers				Shoulders, Smoked				Lemons		
	Loin, Short				Shoulders, Corned				Limes		
	Strip				Tongues				Limes, Florida		
	Shell Strip				Tongues, Beef Smoked				Limes, Persian		
	Ribs Beef				Tongues, Fresh				Muskmelons		
	Shins				Tongues, Lambs				Oranges		
	Suet, Beef				Tripe				Oranges		
	Tails, Ox								Oranges		
	PROVISIONS				Lobsters, Tails				Liederkranz		
	Bacon				Lobsters, Chicken				Parmesan, Grated		
	Bologna				Lobsters, Medium				Roquefort		
	Bologna				Lobsters, Large				Roquefort		
	Crepinette				Oysters, Box				Roquefort, Broken		
	Salami				Oysters, Blue Points				Stilton		
	Hams, Corned				Oysters,				Store		
	Hams, Fresh				Scallops				Swiss		
	Hams, Polish				Shrimps				Swiss, Gruyere		
	Hams, Smoked				Turtle				Swiss, Gruyere		
	Hams, Virginia										
	Hams, Westphalia				**FISH**				Miscellaneous		
	Head Cheese				Bass, Black						
	Lard				Bass, Sea						
	Lyon Sausage				Bass, Striped						
	Phil. Scrapple				Blackfish						
	Smoked Butts				Bluefish						
	Pig's Feet				Bloaters						
	Pig's Heads, Corned				Butterfish						

the various purveyors' names opposite each item, as well as the price each is quoting for that day. At least three purveyors are called for quotations. They know, of course, the hotel's specifications on their particular products, and they know the hotel will check their merchandise to make certain it meets these specifications. Prices are checked each day because the market changes constantly, and because there are times when a purveyor may have made a particularly good buy on a certain item and can pass an improved price on to the hotel. After the steward has obtained three bids on each item, he compares prices, and—delivery, quality, and amount available being equal—buys according to the best price.

The purchasing specification form shown in Figure 17 is used for both purchasing and receiving, and a specification is set for every item purchased. How are these food specifications arrived at? From past experience, but particularly by test and experiment. Of course specifications may vary according to the purpose for which a particular product is desired. And of course they may change, because new products and new ideas continually become known and because a good operation should always try to improve itself. If a new item is tested and found superior to the one being used, a change is therefore made. Many times a change may appear only slight—perhaps just a difference in the way a piece of meat is being cut, but this difference in cut may mean a better portion yield. The change may be the size of oranges or grapefruit being served or in the number of slices in a loaf of bread, and the savings may be only a few cents and may seem like a small matter, but these apparently tiny savings add up to larger profits.

Staple items are generally purchased two or three times a month. For these items a par stock is maintained. Thus, when an item drops below a given amount the quantity necessary to bring it back to par is purchased.

Meat is purchased daily, but three days in advance of when it is to be used, since practically all meat must have some

Strip (Strip Loin or Shell-Bone In)-Top Prime

1. Shell to measure, flat, not more than 1½ inches from the meat on the hip end and not more than 2½ inches from the principal muscle meat on the rib end.

2. Square cut on the ends, no pin bone.

   a. On the hip end, last blade to be split and the cut made per pendicular to the line of the backbone and square with the plane of the cutting table.

3. Good conformation on the back and the fat trimmed to no more than ½ inch of covering.

4. To weigh not less than 15 pounds and not more than 17½ pounds.

5. It is desirable that the strips be as long as possible, preferably selected to 16 inches or more.

6. Strips should be aged not less than 2½ weeks nor more than 4 weeks.

Ribs

1. 7-rib cut, to measure on the flank, no more than 1½ inches from the meat of the main muscle (eye) on the loin end and no more than 4½ from the inside of the chine bone and the chunk end.

   a. Must be cut straight between these two points. CARE SHOULD BE TAKEN TO ENSURE THIS STRAIGHTNESS.

2. White button between ribs, porous bones and clean white fat.

3. Chine bone removed squarely to where the meat splits.

4. To weigh not less than 23 lbs. and not more than 27½ lbs. (Selection of primal ribs weighing 33½-36½ lbs. will ensure this).

5. Ribs should be aged not less than 10 days nor more than 21 days from the date of slaughter.

6. Ribs should not show heavy fat layers on chuck end or along flank, nor should back have heavy fat covering.

FIGURE 17. *Purchase specification.*

preparation by the butcher before it is cooked, and for large banquets there is a great deal of preparation. The amount of meat needed is decided by the chef, who tells the purchaser the amount and the various cuts to order. From that point to the receiving, the purchaser follows the same procedure used in buying other items.

Poultry is bought the same day or one day before it is to be used, depending on the amount needed for banquets. All fresh fish is purchased the day it is to be served. With today's modern food preservation methods a great deal of fish can be bought frozen, therefore making purchasing necessary only two or three times a week.

There are many variations in purchasing methods because of the location and availability of merchandise; however, the above methods are generally accepted procedure.

Receiving. As stated previously, the purchaser also handles the receiving of foods, and once again the specification form (Figure 16) is used. Certainly if the food is bought according to certain standards it should also be received and checked according to them. Every item received is either weighed or counted, depending on the unit of purchase, then it is checked for quality. This is done by eye, so experience in purchasing and receiving plays a very important part. Once the purchasing steward is

FIGURE 18.   *Receiving clerk's daily report.*

NO. 766B

RECEIVING CLERK'S DAILY REPORT   DATE June 1, 19

QUAN.	UNIT	DESCRIPTION	√	UNIT PRICE	AMOUNT	TOTAL AMOUNT	PURCHASE JOURNAL DISTRIBUTION		
							FOOD DIRECT	FOOD STORES	SUNDRIES
		F. Rozzo & Sons							
6 cans		Backfin		3.25	19.50				
3 doz.		SS Crabs		2.50	7.50				
14 lbs.		Ind.Flounder (18)		.28	3.92				
12½ lbs.		Halibut (2)		.55	12.38	43.30	43.30		
		Embassy Groc.							
10 c/s		Tomato Juice 6/10's		3.70	37.00				
10 c/s		Fruit Cocktail 6/10's		8.25	82.50				
6 cans		Anchovies 28		1.75	10.50				
1 gal.		Soy Sauce			1.70	131.70		131.70	
		Embassy Groc.							
1 doz.		Tobasco Sauce 2 oz.			4.00				
5 c/s		Tomato 6/10's		6.25	31.25				
1 c/s		Sardines 50/¼'s			9.50				
1 c/s		Almond Paste 6/5			31.10	75.85		75.85	
		Winant Co.							
250 lbs.		Cherrystones		4.00	10.00				
150 lbs.		Little Necks		3.00	4.50	14.50	14.50		

SIGNATURE

satisfied with the quality and quantity and has checked that the price of the item is the one quoted, he approves the bill. A record of the receipt of the items is made on a receiving sheet, which may be similar to the sample shown in Figure 18. Here, you will notice that the quantities are listed, then the purveyor's name with the items supplied by him, the unit price, the amount, and the total amount. Next is a direct purchase column, and a storeroom column. Almost everything purchased daily is listed in the direct purchase column. These foodstuffs are generally used within twenty-four hours of receiving; they are issued directly to the kitchen and are charged to the food cost of that day. Items listed in the storeroom column are sent to the storeroom for storage and are issued by requisition as needed. The last column —"Sundries"—is for any item received that is neither food nor beverage but which is used by the food department. Examples are cleaning supplies, paper, and china.

A special system is followed for receiving meat, fish, and poultry. All items are listed on the receiving sheet (as is done with other foods), but in addition a meat tag, which is a form of running inventory, is used. This meat tag, as shown by Figure 19, has two identical parts. On each part are a number, the date, the type of meat, the purveyor's name, the price per pound or unit, and the total price. One part of the tag is attached to the piece of meat, and the other part is sent to the food controller. When the meat is used, the food controller receives the tag-half that was attached to the meat and makes the charge to the food cost. Thus the food controller can, at any time, take an inventory of the meat on hand by comparing his copies of the meat tags with those on the unused meat. If a matching tag were missing it would be apparent that the meat had been issued and used but not charged into the food cost. The meat tag also gives a running record of the date the meat was received, which is an aid in using items with the earliest date first, and which prevents keeping meat, fish, and poultry in the refrigerator too long.

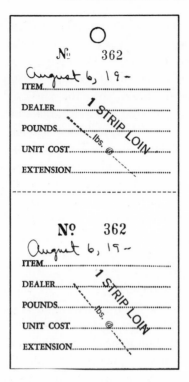

FIGURE 19.   *Meat tag.*

Once the proper food has been purchased and received, the purchasing steward's work is finished.

Storage and Issuance

Food is kept in various types of storage—dry stores; vegetable, dairy, and meat boxes; and freezers. These are under the supervision of the head storeroom man, who takes foods from the receiver and sees to its proper storage. From there the food is issued to the kitchens for preparation.

In any hotel there is a set system for issuing food or anything else that is sent to the kitchen. First, a requisition is written, which must be signed by the executive chef or one of his assistants (see Figure 20). (At no time is food given out without a signed requisition.) These requisitions are then priced by the storeroom man and sent to the food controller. The last day of each month a physical inventory is taken and checked against the requisitions for the month. Two important duties of the head storeroom man are to see that items are issued only by requisition and that the oldest items in the storeroom are used first. Also, the head storeroom man must work closely with the purchaser to keep a small inventory in the storeroom, which avoids accumulating old merchandise, because money tied up in large inventories is not producing revenue. A happy medium must be aimed for; that is, a sufficient inventory should be kept to cover demands, but it must not be so large as to be wasteful.

Preparation

The next phase of food handling takes place in the kitchen, where the food is prepared. The main kitchen, the center of the entire food division, is made up of many small groups.

The butcher shop is one of the most important places in the kitchen, for it is here that the procedure is begun which ultimately results in the entree that is served to a guest. The butcher shop is usually divided into two branches, the meat section and the fish and poultry section, and the duties of the butchers are to prepare for the cooks all meat, fish, and poultry received from the storeroom. The shape and size of a meat entree when it is served is very seldom the same as when the meat was purchased, inasmuch as the serving is cut to specification from a larger piece of meat from which fat and bone have been trimmed. Trimming must be done with the utmost skill, since a hotel pays for the entire piece of meat, including fat and bone which cannot be sold to the guest. Therefore, the butcher must remove just the right amount—enough that the guest will not feel he is being treated unfairly, but not so much that the hotel loses money. If the butcher does his job well, the size of the portion he receives will

			REQUISITION			Nº 975				
			ISSUED TO **KITCHEN DEPT.**							
FROM	M.K.		TO	Help's Hall		DATE	Nov. 30, 19			
QUANTITY	SIZE	LB. WGT.	ARTICLES				UNIT PRICE	AMOUNT TOTAL		
12			Breaded Veal Cutlet					2.	45	
8			Order Fish Cakes						20	
1			Gallon Spaghetti						60	
8			Order Filets of Sole					1.	20	
5			" Finnan Haddie						75	
2			Gallons String Beans					3.	20	
1			" Mashed Potatoes						70	
2		321 lbs	Whole Shoulder of Lamb					10.	00	
2			Gallon Carrots & Peas					3.	00	
						TOTAL				
FORM 716A				SIGNATURE						

FIGURE 20.   *Requisition issued to kitchen department.*

be satisfactory to him and the hotel will maintain its desired food cost.

Every other section of the kitchen has a particular function in preparing food to be served. One section may make cold appetizers and canapés, while another may make salads and desserts. The range section is further subdivided into various groups: one group may make soups, sauces, and gravies; another may take care of roasting and frying; still another may do all broiling; and, during breakfast, the short-order station is manned. In addition, there are people who prepare vegetables for the cooks. It is easily understandable therefore how several people may contribute to the preparation of one dish. A sauce may be made by one cook, to be used on meat roasted by another cook, to be served with a vegetable prepared by a third cook.

Executive Chef. The person responsible for the preparation of all food is the executive chef. However, this responsibility is but one facet of his many duties. Next to the catering manager, the executive chef has a greater variety of duties and a better picture of the food division as a whole than anyone else. The chef's responsibilities begin with the purchasing of the various foods. He must tell the purchasing steward just what he wants and how much he needs; he must check the items when they are received; and he must see that meat is properly cut and prepared so that the best yield and best food possible will be obtained and that the desired food costs will be maintained. In addition, the executive chef writes the menus. This may seem a simple job, but there are several factors which he must always keep in mind at this time: food cost, variety of the menu, a well-balanced workload for the various sections of the kitchen, special days requiring certain dishes, food combinations that will have both taste and visual appeal, and consideration of how items can be used if they are not sold. To aid the executive chef and to relieve him in part of some of his duties, a system known as the "twenty-one-day rotation menu plan" is frequently used in which menus for twenty-one days are continually rotated. In spite of this help the executive chef must still consider special days and make changes to use up leftovers, but rotating menus does eliminate a great deal of paperwork, lowers the food cost, and facilitates purchasing. It is also felt that rotating menus results in better food, since standard recipes are used in the preparation of each item, and the cooks are trained to prepare the various dishes the same way each time.

Although I have only briefly outlined the executive chef's many duties, you should now have some idea of the magnitude of his position. No longer can he be just an expert in food, but he must, as well, have all the other qualifications that make a good executive. The hours an executive chef works are rather long, but a good man can command a very handsome salary and is worth every penny of it to a hotel.

Chief Steward. After the executive chef, the most important person in the kitchen is the chief steward. The duties of the chief steward cover all phases of kitchen operation, with the exception of actual food preparation. Normally, food preparation and service is handled separately for the public restaurant and for banquets, and for each operation the chief steward has assistants whose duties may vary somewhat. The floor chef, in the main kitchen, bears overall responsibility for dishwashing and kitchen cleanliness. The banquet steward has very few regular workers, but their duty is to set up banquets (this involves taking silver, glass, china, and other equipment to the banquet rooms so the waiters can set the tables). Almost all of the warewashers are hired as extras and therefore require a great deal of supervision. The chief steward is responsible for the payroll of his groups, and he must schedule their work very carefully in order not to be overstaffed; here he can use the forecast and staffing guide to great advantage. China, glass, and other equipment are purchased by the chief steward, and by doing an efficient job he can save a great deal of money for the hotel. In addition, he always tries to find better ways for washing dishes and strives to cut down on the breakage and silver loss.

Although there are many other people and positions in the kitchen which could be treated in great detail, I am, as previously stated, covering only the better known positions that are most likely to be found in any hotel regardless of its size.

Selling and Service

The banquet department represents one of the most important areas of a hotel's food operation, and within this department are two distinct divisions: selling, and service. Each depends greatly upon the other, and both must work hand in hand for a successful overall department.

Sales. The person in charge of banquet sales is usually referred to as the banquet manager. Within the sales division ther are several sales representatives who do the actual selling of banquets, weddings, dances, cocktail parties, or other social events. Their duties are the same as those of any other salesman —in establishing contacts they write letters, make telephone calls, conduct personal visits, and follow up leads that have been furnished by various sources. The sales representatives have both tangible and intangible products to sell. The tangibles are food, beverages, and function space; the intangibles are service and good will. It goes without saying that a hotel sales staff must have some knowledge of food and beverages if it is to sell these things, and it must know how rooms are set up for different functions. The staff must also be able to originate new ideas in regard to arrangements and menus. But most important, anyone engaged in hotel sales work must be able to sell himself and in doing so gain the complete confidence of the guest.

Hotel sales people work with such tools as set menus, price lists of various items, and floor plans with sample setups. Once a suitable date and time for a function is decided by a guest, the sales representative must make menu and beverage suggestions. When a final decision is reached, an agreement is drawn up which gives all necessary information: menu, price, table arrangements, and the number of people expected (see Figures 21A and 21B). The agreement is signed in duplicate by the guest, who is given a copy, and the original is placed in the hotel's file.

A week before the function this information is typed on the menu (see Figure 21C), which is sent around to the hotel personnel who are concerned with function operations; in addition, a floor plan is sent to the banquet headwaiter to enable him to instruct his housemen in the table setups. Two days before the function the sales representative checks with the guest for any

WEDDING ____________

DANCE ____________

____________ DATE ____________

This is an Agreement with ____________

____________ AND THE ____________ HOTEL.

THIS FUNCTION WILL BE HELD IN THE ____________ ROOM.

DAY ______ DATE ______ MONTH ______ 195__ TIME ______ A.M. P.M.

BULLETIN AS FOLLOWS: ____________

ORGANIZATION OR SPONSOR ____________

CHAIRMAN ____________ PHONE ______ BUSINESS | ______ HOME

ADDRESS ____________

NO. EXPECTED	GUARANTEED	PER COVER	RENTAL	DEPOSIT

1. All displays on exhibit if any, must conform to city code fire ordinance rules.
2. All liquors must be purchased from the ____________ Hotel.
3. Terms of this agreement call for payment on completion of the function, unless credit has been previously arranged with our credit department.
4. For private dinners, etc., a guarantee of the lowest number of guests will be required not later than forty-eight hours preceding the affair. We shall be prepared to take care of about ten percent over the guarantee.
5. The Hotel is not to be held responsible if through a strike or a walk out it is unable to fulfill this agreement.
6. Musicians must be Union members.
7. The Hotel reserves the right to assign another room to your group should we for unforseen reason be unable to give you the above named room.

Please sign and return second and third copies. Retain original for your file.

For The ____________ Hotel.

Very truly yours,

____
BANQUET DEPT.

THIS AGREEMENT WAS SUBMITTED ON ______ DATE ACCEPTED BY ______ SIGNATURE

ORIGINAL

FIGURE 21A. *Banquet agreement.*

last-minute changes and also finds out the exact number of persons expected. The guest must guarantee this number, and usually from 5 percent to 10 percent more places are set. No changes can be made later than twenty-four hours before the party time, because of the difficulties involved in preparing the food and hiring extra waiters. The day of the function the sales representative who booked it checks the function room to make certain that it is set according to plan and that all other details such as flowers and checkroom and restroom facilities are in order. It is of utmost importance that when the host-guest arrives the sales representative meet him, show him the room, and re-check any last minute details in order to assure him that

Trace_____

SALES DEPARTMENT BOOKING ORDER

DEFINITE ☐
TENTATIVE ☐   DATE OF CONTACT_____
OPTION UNTIL_____

ORGANIZATION NAME_____   Day of Function_____

PRINCIPAL CONTACT_____   DATE OF FUNCTION_____

ADDRESS_____   PHONE NUMBER_____

TYPE OF FUNCTION_____   ROOM_____
NUMBER PERSONS EXPECTED_____ GUARANTEE_____ TIME OF SERVICE_____
TYPE OF SET UP_____
RENTAL $_____   PER PLATE_____
BAR INFO — CASH ☐ GUARANTEE $_____   OPEN BAR_____

THE FOLLOWING EQUIPMENT WILL BE NECESSARY —

Registration Desk_____	Ashtrays_____	Flowers_____
Tables_____	Ice Water and Glasses_____	Check Room_____
Floor Plan_____	Movie Screen_____	Cigars and Cigarettes_____
Speakers' Platform_____	Projector_____	Miscellaneous_____
Lectern_____	Operator_____	_____
Microphone_____	Spotlight_____	_____
Easel_____	Runway_____	_____
Blackboard, Pointer, Chalk_____	Music_____	_____

MENU ON REVERSE SIDE   Booked By
ORIGINAL   **THIS FORM MUST BE MADE OUT IN TRIPLICATE**

FIGURE 21B. *Sales department booking order.*

everything possible has been done to ensure the success of the party. After the function, on either the same day or the following day, the sales representative contacts the host to find out if he was pleased with the results and to ask if he would like to reserve the same date and room again.

This following up is becoming more and more important to hotels, not only because of the great competition between hotels themselves, but also because the various types of clubs are catering to private parties. Many of the large hotels now hire specialists for particular selling—conventions, shows (such as drug shows and shoe exhibits), showers, weddings. It should be noted that wedding parties represent a very good source of

Name
Address
Phone

Arrangements
Made By

Character of Function, Room

Day, Date, Time

MENU	ADDITIONAL DETAILS

This function to be classified and marked on the check as
Breakfast ☐   Lunch ☐   Dinner ☐   Supper ☐

Number To Prepare For

Number Guaranteed   Number Served

Price Per Cover   Deposit

Check No.   Banquet Manager

File	Banqu. Manag.	Banqu. Headw.	Cater. Manag.	Food Contr.	Chief Acct.	Head Checker	Purch. Agent	Chef No. 1	Chef No. 2	Pastry Chef	Butcher	Kitchen Stew.	Wine Stew.

FIGURE 21C.   *Sales department menu.*

income to a hotel on such days when other functions are not available, particularly on weekends, when there is little or no commercial business.

Service.   Once a function is booked and all "selling" arrangements have been made, the banquet service group takes

over. As mentioned before, the headwaiter recieves a floor plan
from which he instructs the housemen how to set up the room.
From the menu he gets information regarding the type of service
and the number of people attending, and this lets him know how
many extra waiters to hire. The headwaiter also checks the menu
for such things as wine to be served with the meal, flowers,
liquor, and he notes whether or not there are to be after-dinner
speakers, a movie, or anything special that may alter the service
arrangements. When all of these details are settled, he must make
up table schedules for the waiters; for this he uses copies of the
floor plan on which each table is numbered.

Waiters are assigned various stations in pairs of usually one
regular waiter and one extra waiter. The regular waiter knows
where the china, glass, and silver are kept, the way the tables are
to be set up, and the type of service demanded by the headwaiter. By being paired, the regular waiter can aid the extra one,
and much better guest service will result. You may ask: If extra
waiters create a problem, why not have more regular waiters?
The answer to this is payroll control. On one day the banquet
department may serve 3,000 covers, and on the next day it may
serve 300 covers. To stabilize such situations a hotel has on its
payroll regular extra waiters. These waiters get first call for all
functions in the hotel, and if others are needed, they are hired
through the union.

The headwaiter has a most important job and is responsible
for a great variety of duties. In addition to supervising the setting
up of the room, he must make sure that the banquet steward has
the proper type and sufficient amounts of glass, china, and silver
available for the party. He must determine that linen has been
reserved from the laundry, and that each waiter is handling his
station properly. He must coordinate with the host any late
changes, check the arrival of flowers, and take note of any little
details that may cause the dinner to begin late or disturb the
guests. He must work very closely with the chef in order to let
him know when the service will begin and the actual number of

people to be served. Once the service of the banquet begins, he tells the waiters when to pick up soiled dishes and when to serve the next course. If there is to be a movie after the dinner he makes sure that someone is standing by to turn off the lights. The headwaiter must stay until the conclusion of a function to look after all the guests' desires and finally to have the host sign the check. He must plan the work of his housemen well, because often one room will be used two or three times in a day, or several setups may be necessary during one gathering with a minimum of time available for making such changes. Planning ahead and arranging setups that can be changed easily saves extra work and cuts payroll costs. It should now be evident that the greatest asset of a well-run banquet group is complete cooperation among all departments and department heads. The executive chef and the headwaiter, the chief steward and the headwaiter—none can do his own job really well without the aid of the others.

Also in the service group are the people in charge of the various restaurants in a hotel. They are generally known as headwaiters, hosts, or hostesses, and their jobs are basically the same in all of the dining rooms—they act as hosts for the hotel by seating guests and seeing that the guests receive good service. To this end, service employee classes at which the menu is discussed are held before each meal. If new items appear on the menu, the host explains how these are prepared. The host discusses the service, giving instructions on how certain dishes are to be served and what silver is necessary, and also discusses any special questions. Uniforms are checked to make sure everyone looks fresh and clean. If waiters or waitresses have any problems which they feel may hinder service they tell the host, and should another department be involved the host speaks to that department head in order to clear up the matter. During the course of service the host makes certain that each table is set according to house policy. He checks salt and pepper shakers and the sugar bowls for cleanliness and fullness, and he sees that ashtrays are kept clean. He inspects all glasses and silverware for spots, and watches for torn table linen. He watches that the waiters or waitresses are giving proper attention to their stations and not talking to one another. He notes any criticisms or suggestions and passes them on to the catering manager. It is necessary that the host work closely with the chef, for in this way he can lower food costs by making sure that the waiters return any usable food to the kitchen. Also the host aids the chief steward by lessening breakage and silver losses—proper stacking of china and glassware not only minimizes the possibility of breakage but also makes the dishwasher's job easier. He also checks that all silver is removed from the table before the linen is picked up. Last, but far from least, the host in the restaurant is one of the hotel's best salesmen, for he comes into contact with the guest and hears his desires, likes, and dislikes. The host must be diplomatic, and a wide-awake person who is well liked can do an outstanding job of increasing the business of a restaurant.

THE BEVERAGE FUNCTION

Purchasing and Receiving

Mainly responsible for the beverage division of the catering department are the wine steward and the head bartender. The wine steward handles the purchasing and receiving of beverages, which is a simpler process than its counterpart in the food division. The beverage industry is a highly regulated one. Liquor is packaged in certain size bottles, and standards must be met in order to comply with federal regulations, therefore, the federal government, through its laws, has made liquor buying relatively easy. When a fifth of liquor is purchased and a certain size drink is poured from it consistently, it is a simple matter to know just how many drinks will be obtained, regardless of the brand or from whom it was purchased. In purchasing food this surety is not true: a twenty-two pound strip loin purchased from one purveyor might yield one more steak than the same size loin from another purveyor. The purchase price of liquor is also regulated, in varying degrees, by the state governments. In some states liquor can be purchased only through state-owned stores, and of course the price is fixed by the state. In other states liquor prices must be filed two months in advance by the purveyors. Therefore, in most instances there is no point in shopping for a better price. The actual problem in buying liquor is to know what the guests will want and what they are willing to pay. It is practical to buy only what is needed for a given period in order to prevent building up too large an inventory, since all liquor is sold on a cash basis and stock lying in the wine room is not producing income. Some shopping can be done for beverages that are used in cocktails and other mixed drinks, inasmuch as it is possible to use with them a lesser known brand of liquor which will be just as acceptable as a highly advertised, more expensive brand. Taste tests are often made to determine the best brand at the best price. A par stock of liquor is maintained in the wine room, and most hotels buy either once or twice a month, whichever best suits their demands, to replenish this stock. Therefore the wine steward need only check his bin cards to see what is needed, and the orders are then given to the catering manager, who does the actual buying. Decisions in regard to ordering new items and changing brands are usually made by the catering manager, the general manager, and the head bartender together.

The receiving of beverages is, like the purchasing, a straight-forward process. After the order is placed, the requisition is returned to the wine steward with the prices and amounts of the various brands ordered. When the liquor is received he checks the invoice against the requisition for price and quantity. He also checks the number of cases and makes sure that there are no broken bottles. A receiving sheet (see Figure 22) records the information, and the receiving sheet and invoices are sent to the

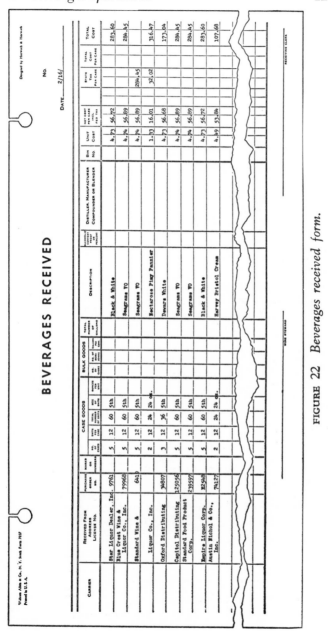

FIGURE 22 *Beverages received form.*

food and beverage controller. The wine steward stamps the bin number for a particular brand on each bottle, and the bottles are placed in the bin.

Storage and Issuance

All liquor and wine is stored in the wine room or wine cellar and is issued by a requisition (Figure 23), which must be made out and signed by either the head bartender or the catering manager. A par stock is maintained at the bars that serve the various restaurants. When a bar closes each day, all empty bottles are sent to the wine room, and the next day a full bottle is sent to the

FIGURE 23.   *Wine cellar requisition.*

List No.	Qts.	Pts.	Spl.		DESCRIPTION	Unit Cost		Total	
	9				Ballantine Scotch				
	12				Deluxe Stagg				
	12				Stodarts Scotch				
	12				Fleischmans Gin				
	2				J. Walker Black				
	4				J. Walker Red				
	6				Haig & Haid 5 Star				
	3				Martins VVO				
	6				Teachers Highland Cream				
		1 c/s			Miller High Life				
		1 c/s			Budweiser Beer				
		1 c/s			Schlitz Beer				
		6 c/s			Club Soda Canada Dry				
		4 c/s			Ginger Ale Canada Dry				

WINE CELLAR REQUISITION № 2980

PLEASE DELIVER TO **BANQUET SERVICE BAR** DATE 11/1/- 19

DEPARTMENT

RECEIVED_____ **BANQUET SERVICE BAR**

DEPARTMENT

BY_____

bar to replace each empty returned the previous day; therefore approximately the same number of bottles is always at the bar. A requisition is made up for each replacement bottle, but the bin number is used instead of brand name and size, as each number corresponds to certain bottles. At the banquet bar no par stock is maintained—liquor is issued only as it is needed. There, the head bartender must obtain a copy of the banquet menu and from it determine the liquor required. At the same time he must check to see if any extra bartenders will be needed. For the banquet bars, a different colored liquor requisition form is used, but the bin numbers remain the same. Requisitions covering liquor needed for banquet bars include not only the amount needed but also the room and the time the beverage is to be there.

Preparation

It is the responsibility of the head bartender to see that all drinks are mixed properly and also to maintain the beverage cost at the percentage decided upon by the management. He must work closely with the beverage controller, since continual testing is necessary and a physical inventory must be taken every ten days.

Selling and Service

Beverages are sold and served by the host or hostess, waiter or waitress, and bartenders, and a great deal can be accomplished by each toward stimulating the sale of beverages. At the briefing session before a meal the special drink for the day and the way it is to be served are discussed. In a room where wine can be sold, the host and captain are trained to suggest wines with a meal once a guest has ordered. Sales can also be increased greatly if the waiter or waitress suggests a cocktail before dinner and, when dinner is being served, suggests a bottle of wine which will go with the dinner. The guest who has a cocktail before dinner is always a fine prospect for wine with the dinner itself. To aid the waiters and waitresses in selling wines, wine promotion classes are held three or four times a year. At these classes an expert discusses various types of wine, how they taste, and what type of dish they are best served with. After the talk, wines are tasted by the class to give them a better idea of the products they are trying to sell. It has been found that after such classes wine sales actually do increase. Of course this is just one of many methods, but *every* employee should be encouraged to contribute ideas that will help to boost sales.

FOOD AND BEVERAGE CONTROL

The Food Controller—General Duties

Food and beverage control is a particular form of accounting used exclusively by the food and beverage divisions. You will note from the organization chart (Figure 15) that the food and beverage controller is responsible only to the catering manager and has no one under him. His main job is to supply information to the other department heads. He gathers information and from it makes suggestions to various people, but it is up to the catering manager to decide if these suggestions should be put into effect. This does not minimize the importance of the food controller's position, inasmuch as food prices are always changing much faster than the menu prices can be adjusted to meet them, and any suggestions the food controller has which will cut costs on various items and help to maintain profits are always welcomed. It should be noted though that a good food cost is not only the food controller's job, but that of everyone in the food department. Those who cut, cook, or serve are the people who can make the real savings. The food controller can keep the records, gather information, and make suggestions, but it is up to the department heads to *utilize* this valuable information.

The food controller, like most other department heads within the food division of the catering department, has a great variety of duties. Some are directly related to food and others are "second cousins," but all are important to the overall success of the operation.

Forecasting

One of the most important questions in regard to food and beverage control is: How many covers will we serve next week? The right answer almost automatically ensures a good food and payroll cost. The food controller tries to provide the right answer by forecasting. The system employed to arrive at a final forecast is not a form of magic; it is simply the gathering of facts and figures for a given period of time, from which a factor is determined based on the number of covers served in ratio to the number of people in the hotel.

By applying a little common sense, one can, for example, determine the number of covers to be served in the coffee shop on Tuesday for breakfast: Assume that the food controller uses a factor of .4 for breakfast covers in the coffee shop. The house count is 1,400, but the banquet office has given information that a group of 200 people staying in the hotel will have breakfast in one of the banquet rooms. From this information a preliminary forecast can be made as follows.

House count	1,400
Less banquet	200
	1,200
Factor	.4
Covers to be served	480

A forecast made a week in advance could, of course, become obsolete, but this is just a preliminary forecast (see Figure 24). Every day, the food controller adjusts the three-day forecast, as

FORECAST ANNOUNCEMENT

ANNUAL SEQUENCE NO. 42
FOR DEPT. HEAD MEETING

Fri 19 Day
Date

I. ROOM OCCUPANCY

NIGHT OF: (USE PRIOR NIGHT)	Thursday 99	Friday 98	Saturday 94	Sunday 94	Monday 99	Tuesday 99	Wednesday 99	Thursday 98	Friday 93	Saturday 88	Sunday 90
CAL.DATE:	10/18	10/19	10/20	10/21	10/22	10/23	10/24	10/25	10/26	10/27	10/28
FORECAST:	R-1436 / O-1590	1,422 / 1,580	1,364 / 1,670	1,364 / 1,670	1,436 / 1,610	1,436 / 1,590	1,436 / 1,580	1,422 / 1,570	1,233 / 1,400	1,277 / 1,570	1,306 / 1,610

RESULTS, LAST 7 DAYS: (NOTE: * ASTERISK INDICATES FIGURES THAT WERE REVISED)

Rooms 9,691   99 % Occ.   93.8 % Occ.

FINAL FCST.	(1,291)	(1,393)	(1,422)	(1,248)	(1,422)	(1,422)	(1,422)	(1,422)-(9,620)-(93.1)
ACTUAL ACC.	(1,347)	(1,332)	(1,448)	(1,174)	(1,445)	(1,447)	(1,450)	(1,450)-(9,643)-(93.3)
DIFFERENCE (Actual + or -)	(46)	(41)	(. 26)	(74)	(23)	(25)	(28)	(28)-(23)-(.2)

TOTAL % Occ.

REMARKS:

II. FOOD COVERS BY ROOMS: (CORRESPONDING DAY)

	Sunday	Monday	Tuesday	Wednesday	Thursday	Friday	Saturday	Week
MAIN DINING ROOM	70	110	115	130	105	95	50	675
ROOM SERVICE	420	390	405	470	450	410	420	2,965
BANQUET (BUFFETS @ EACH)	285	610	115	125	585	75	550	2,545
GREEN ROOM	40	100	110	105	110	80	65	610
BEIGE ROOM	640	665	820	790	670	660	535	4,780
SUB TOTAL	1,455	2,075	1,565	1,620	1,920	1,320	1,620	11,575
OTHER: (@ EACH) DRUG STORE	875	1,300	1,400	1,400	1,425	1,250	950	8,500
TOTAL COVERS	2,330	3,375	2,965	3,020	3,245	2,570	2,570	20,075
RESULTS LAST WEEK: FORECAST # COVERS	2,385	3,235	3,615	3,030	3,210	2,770	3,025	21,270
ACTUAL # SERVED	2,593	2,961	3,625	3,517	3,089	2,803	2,718	21,306
DIFFERENCE (ACTUAL + or -)	208	274	10	487	121	33	307	36
							% Diff.	1.6

REMARKS:

shown by the example in Figure 25. Therefore, information is sent out not only a week in advance, but three days before, and finally the day before, which is as close as most departments could wish. The final figure is, then, only as accurate as the information used. Factors are developed from the previous year's record of covers served and house count and are constantly checked to maintain accuracy, with necessary adjustments being made. Other facts to be taken into consideration when determining the number of people who will be served are the weather and the day itself. On Friday, the dinner count is usually small because most travelers are on their way home. On Sunday, lunch business is off because the majority of people in hotels usually eat a late breakfast and an early dinner and skip lunch. There are other considerations, and each hotel will have its own explanation for the rise and fall of covers. While any hotel can use the method outlined above for forecasting, each must necessarily arrive at its own factors. Now, let us consider some of the most important reasons for the forecast and the people who actually use it.

Every group head in the food division uses the forecast. First, it is used for staffing the various groups. As examples, the headwaiter utilizes the forecast to determine how many waiters and busboys will be required, and the chef decides, with the aid of the forecast, the number of cooks and pantry people he must have. It is essential that the correct number of people be hired— enough to get the job done well, but not more than are actually needed. Next, the forecast is used in determining the amounts of food to purchase, and the necessary quantities of linen, silver, and china. The chef uses the forecast to ascertain how much food should be prepared; therefore, it is probably one of the greatest aids in maintaining low food costs. Over-production is a chief deterrent to achieving proper food costs, and the forecast eliminates, to a great extent, the possibility of it. The purchaser uses the forecast in order to purchase as near as possible the amount of food needed for a given period of time, thus reducing the chance

DAY & DATE		WED. 12/5	THURS. 12/6	FRI. 12/7
ROOMS OCCUPANCY		1,422	1,422	1,306
OCCUPANCY %		98	98	90
GUEST COUNT		1,625	1,620	1,575
ROUGE ROOM	L	80	60	60
	D	70	60	60
	T	150	120	120
ROOM SERVICE	B	215	220	210
	L	60	90	85
	D	175	160	160
	T	450	470	455
GREEN ROOM	L	60	60	40
	D	60	55	65
	T	120	115	105
BEIGE ROOM	B	430	410	375
	L	200	180	195
	D	160	170	155
	T	790	760	625
BANQUET REC.		480	535	180
SPECIAL				10
BUFFET				
TOTAL		480	535	190
M. K. TOTAL		1,990	2,000	1,495
FOUNTAIN		1,200	1,275	1,250
GRAND TOTAL		3,190	3,275	2,745

FIGURE 25. *Daily forecast.*

of spoilage. The catering manager can use the information provided by the forecast for planning other purchases. By knowing the approximate income to expect, expenses can be determined and a profit figure arrived at which will tell him what amounts can be expended. The food controller checks his forecast figure against the actual number of covers served (see Figure 24). If he is setting a trend of over or under forecasting, he adjusts his factors accordingly.

If forecasting appears difficult, it should be thought of as little more than the gathering of facts and figures over a given period of time that will set a pattern. In this respect it is very much like a baseball player's batting average: against one pitcher a player may hit .400, but against another pitcher in a different park he may hit .200. The same principle is characteristically true of covers served per room count: on a Monday in July a different number of covers may be served than on a Thursday in December.

The *daily* forecast is the basis for all forecasts, whether they be weekly, monthly, or yearly. With the trend to more chain-operated hotels, forecasting income and expense for the year is a common practice. There may be some question as to why the home office of a chain requests forecasts from its hotels a year in advance. There are many reasons, but one of the most important is to provide the home office with information that may be utilized in expansion plans. For a chain to continue to prosper it must keep growing. If the board of directors has a sound idea of how much profit will be made in the coming year, it knows how much money can be spent on growth and still return a dividend to the stockholders. This points up, too, how important to the overall picture such a relatively simple thing as a daily forecast can be.

Food Costs and Sales

As mentioned before, the chief duties of the food controller are gathering data and compiling information to be sent to various departments for their own use. Where does this data come from and where or to whom is it sent? Figure 26, a summary of food costs and potential savings, should clarify this. We will review this form item by item and discuss the origin of the information, who receives copies of the summary, and what use is made of it.

Three items are listed in the upper right-hand corner of the summary. The date, the day of the week, and the weather are factors that can influence the amount of business that will be done, and this information is supplied daily for each new summary sheet by the food controller. The body of the report is divided into two major columns: "Today" refers to the date that appears in the upper right-hand corner; "To-Date" refers to cumulative days to that date in that month. These latter two columns are further broken down as follows.

Number Sold (often called "covers") is guests served. The waiter or waitress writes, at the top of each dinner check, the number of persons served. The dinner checks are turned in daily to the night auditor, and one of his assistants, the restaurant controller, gets the cover count for all of the dining rooms from the night restaurant report. Of what value is this information? First, it gives the actual number of guests served, which is compared with the forecasted number and is used in making up later forecasts. Secondly, it is used to determine the amount of the average check, which, it will be recalled, is used to forecast dollar income. These are the two most important uses of the cover count information, but there are others—such as determining turnover in the various dining rooms. The checks are also time stamped, which enables an estimate of high and low volume periods; this, in turn, aids in staffing and food preparation. And the checks are used for comparisons with last week and/or last year and are carefully watched if price adjustments are made or a new type of menu is introduced in one of the restaurants.

Actual Sales is the dollar income from the day's covers. This information also is obtained from the dinner checks and the night

	SUMMARY OF FOOD COSTS AND POTENTIAL SAVINGS				DATE 12/9			
TO:					DAY			
					WEATHER			
	TO-DAY				**TO-DATE**			
	NUMBER SOLD	ACTUAL SALES	CALCULATED COST	COST PER DOLLAR SALE	NUMBER SOLD	ACTUAL SALES	CALCULATED COST	COST PER DOLLAR SALE
ROOM SERVICE								
BREAKFAST								
LUNCH								
DINNER								
A LA CARTE ENTRE								
A LA CARTE OTHERS								
TOTAL	1,501	3,233 00			4,172	9,481 55		
ROOM								
BREAKFAST								
LUNCH								
DINNER								
A LA CARTE ENTRE								
A LA CARTE OTHERS								
TOTAL	2,478	4,305 85			6,193	10,522 25		
ROOM								
LUNCH								
DINNER								
A LA CARTE ENTRE								
A LA CARTE OTHERS								
TOTAL	312	1,142 70			928	3,379 30		
ROOM								
LUNCH								
DINNER								
A LA CARTE ENTRE								
A LA CARTE OTHERS								
TOTAL	267	654 75			824	1,949 05		
LOUNGE		72 85				150 35		
POTENTIAL NET COST ALL REST'S	4,558	9,409 15	2,813 89	29.9	12,117	25,482 50	7,840 66	20.8
BANQUETS	1,076	6,005 10	1,594	26.5	3,719	22,009 20	5,694 21	25.9
POTENTIAL NET COST M. K.	5,634	15,114 25	4,534 20	30.0	15,836	47,491 70	14,247 30	30.0
ACTUAL NET COST M. K.	5,634	15,114 25	4,407 89	28.6	15,836	47,491 70	13,534 87	28.5
POTENTIAL SAVING M. K.			126 31	1.4			712 43	1.4
FOUNTAIN								
POTENTIAL NET COST	3,036	1,559 47	585 80	37.5	9,640	4,655 01	1,745 63	37.5
ACTUAL NET COST			525 51	33.7			1,736 54	37.3
POTENTIAL SAVING			59 29	3.8			9 09	.2
SUMMARY								
GROSS COST-ACTUAL	8,670	16,973 72	5,531 63	32.6	25,476	52,146 71	17,500 93	33.6
LESS EMPLOYEE MEALS			598 23	3.5			2,229 52	4.3
NET COST ACTUAL			4,933 40	29.1			15,271 41	29.3
NET COST POTENTIAL			5,595 66	33.0			16,659 94	31.9
TOTAL POTENTIAL SAVINGS			662 26	3.9			1,388 53	2.6

FIGURE 26. *Summary of food costs and sales.*

auditor's report. It is used in conjunction with the cover count to determine the average check, to guide in watching for increased or decreased sales, or to make any other calculations for which the average check is used, except, of course, it is reported in dollars instead of in cover count. Total sales is also used in determining food cost percentage.

Calculated Cost is just what the name implies—the calculated or estimated cost of the food sold in the restaurant. It is arrived at by analyzing the checks for the day.

Cost per Dollar Sale is more often referred to as food cost. It is arrived at by dividing the cost of food by dollar sales.

We will not discuss the items that appear under the various restaurants listed along the left-hand side of the summary inasmuch as these entries are self explanatory. Information for the three entries under Fountain (near the bottom of Figure 26) is obtained and used in the same manner as is that for the entries under Summary, which are discussed below.

Gross Cost is the cost of all food used during the day, whether it is sold to a guest or used in the employees' cafeteria, and it is entered in the "Today" column. This information comes from three sources: (1) the direct purchases—from the discussion of the receiving sheet (Figure 18), direct purchases are foodstuffs which are used within a twenty-four hour period and which are charged into that day's food cost; (2) the meat tags—the meat tags (Figure 19), placed on a piece of meat when it is received, are sent to the food controller to be charged to that day's food cost when the meat is issued for preparation; (3) requisitions written and signed by the chef—these requisitions, used in drawing food from the storeroom, are priced and sent to the food controller to be charged to that day's food cost. By totaling the figures from these sources, we arrive at the gross food cost. This is a figure as close to the actual cost of the food as can be obtained without taking a daily inventory, and it is usually within ½ percent of the actual figure.

Employee Meals is the cost of food used to feed the hotel

employees, and it is arrived at from information from the chef. All food sent to the employees' cafeteria is issued by requisitions. The requisitions are priced at cost, and the food controller then subtracts the total amount from gross cost, which gives the net cost.

Net Cost Actual is the cost of the food sold, which, in turn, means food sold in the restaurant.

Net Cost Potential is the cost estimated for the month, or the goal attempted in relation to food cost. The difference between net cost and potential cost is excess cost or potential savings. In the "Today" column this figure will fluctuate almost daily; however, in the "To-Date" column it will be rather consistent. Notice that a potential net cost is forecast for all restaurants and for the main kitchen. Should net cost actual in the summary be excessively high or low, the potential net cost figures will help management pinpoint the problem area. Of course there can be various reasons for a difference between net cost actual and net cost potential. For example, in Figure 26, net cost potential is 2.6 percent higher than net cost actual. This is because the report is for the first nine days of the month and a great deal of food in production inventory at the close of the previous month's business is still being used.

To repeat, the summary report is made up daily by the food controller and is distributed by him to the pertinent people. The food controller also handles other reports that are put out periodically, most of them coming at the end of the month when inventories are taken, which enables him to arrive at actual costs for the month. One of these reports (a reconciliation of food costs), made for the monthly closing, is shown in Figure 27.

Reconciliation of Food Costs

Most of the items in the reconciliation form are self explanatory. The storeroom inventory is obtained by taking an actual physical

```
        RECONCILIATION OF BEVERAGE COST FOR MONTH OF    November

   Opening Wine Room Inventory       $ 53062.20
   Opening Bar Inventory               4392.13
        Total Opening Inventory      $ 57454.33

   Beverage Purchases                $ 42710.15
   Food to Bars                          457 55
        Total Charges                              $100,622.03


   Less:
   Closing Wine Room Inventory       $ 65658.97
   Closing Bar Inventory               4924.32
        Total Closing Inventory      $ 70583.29

   Less:
   Stewards Sales Chgd. to SCA           31.42
   Employees Relations                   28.24
   Steward Sales                       1162.96
   Beverage to Food                      60.92
   Cook's Beer                          524.43
   Cost of Promotion Sales              436.18
        Total Credits                $  2244.15
        Total All Credits                          $ 72,827.44
                                                                     %
   Cost of Beverage Sold                            $ 27,794.59    34.5

   Less:  Employees Meals

   Net Cost of Beverage Sold


   Recap of Storeroom Issues
   Employees Relations               $     4.29
   All Bars (Food excluded)            19677.13
   Full Bottles                         8642.04
   Cook's Beer                          523.23
   Beverage to Food                       48.81
   Steward Sales                        1158.67
   Entertainment & Promotion              52.63
        Total Book Issues            $ 30106.80
        Total Actual Issues            30113.28
           Over or Short Issue       $     6.48


   Total Sales  $ 80,614.16
```

FIGURE 27.   *Reconciliation of food cost.*

count of the items and pricing them. Production inventory is the food in the kitchen which has been issued from the storeroom during the month, or food from direct purchase. Beverage to food is any wine used in cooking, the cost of which is transferred from beverage cost to food cost. Food to bars is a transfer from food cost to beverage cost of items used in making up drinks—items such as oranges, lemons, sugar, and eggs. Gratis to bars is also a transfer from food to beverage, but it differs from food to bars in that it is food *given* to the guest—potato chips, peanuts, canapés, hors d'oeuvres. Grease sales, garbage sales, and rebates are self-explanatory. Cost of promotion sales are costs of food used for promoting business, and would include buying lunch for a potential customer. Such checks are not picked up in the daily sales figure, but are written off at the end of the month at cost. Steward sales cover any food sold (usually at cost) to anyone anyplace other than in the restaurants or employees' cafeteria. An example of this would be the food used for an office party. The item Cash Sales—Employees' Meals is explained by the fact that not all employees who eat in the cafeteria are entitled to free meals; some must pay the cost price for them. This payment is cash sales and is credited to the cost of employees' meals. The next five items we have already discussed. The recap of storeroom issues is a check on the accuracy of the requisitions during the month. The figure opposite the title Total Book Issues is a total of requisitions presented to the storeroom during the month. Total actual issues are arrived at with the aid of the physical inventory. As an example,

Opening storeroom inventory	$1,111.11
plus storeroom purchases	1,111.11
Total available	$2,222.22
Less closing storeroom inventory	1,111.11
Total actual issue	$1,111.11

The difference between book issue and actual issue is the overage or shortage. This figure should be as close to zero as possible. When it is, it assures a tight control on the storeroom's issues.

A similar report is issued for liquor, and it contains the same information (see Figure 28, and Figure 29—an analysis of bever-

RECONCILIATION OF FOOD COST FOR THE MONTH OF   November

Opening Storeroom Inventory	$ 7009.71		
Opening Production Inventory	3676.36		
Total Opening Inventory	$ 10686.07		
Storeroom Purchases	$ 45778.72		
Direct Purchases	20462.42		
Total Purchases	$ 66241.14		
Beverage to Food	$ 60.92		
Total Charges		$ 76988.13	
Less:			
Closing Storeroom Inventory	$ 10450.96		
Closing Direct Inventory	4424.57		
Total Closing Inventory	$ 14875.53		
Less:			
Food to Bars	$ 457.55		
Grease Sales	43.91		
Gratis to Bars	477.55		
Steward Sales Chgd. to SCA	74.26		
Cost of Promotion Sales	333.53		
Steward Sales	166.06		
Employees Rel.	1093.09		
Cash Sales-Employees Meals	2055.55		
Total Credits	$ 4701.50		
Total All Credits		$ 19577.33	%
Gross Cost of Food Consumed		$ 57410.80	35.6
Less: Employees Meals		8368.85	5.2
Net Cost of Food Sold		$ 49041.95	30.4
Potential Net Cost of Food Sold		51582.19	32.0
Potential Savings		$ 2540.24	1.6
Recap of Storeroom Issues:			
Main Kitchen	$ 37506.60		
Food to Bars	280.25		
Food to Buffet	252.55		
Steward Sales			
Entertainment & Promotion			
Cafeteria	1173.30		
Drug Store	3080.75		
Total Book Issues		$ 42293.45	
Total Actual Issues		42337.47	
Storeroom - Over or (Short)		$ 44.02	
Total Sales $ 161,242.25			

FIGURE 28.   *Reconciliation of beverage cost.*

age sales and costs). These two reports are among the most important ones issued by the food controller.

Food Testing

Another important duty the food controller performs is making tests of yields and checking portion sizes in order to give the best possible merchandise at the best price. Here, he must work very closely with the chef. The yield chart shown in Figures 30A and

	Combined Operations	GREEN ROOM BAR	BANQUET BAR	LOUNGE	
November 19 –		ANALYSIS OF BEVERAGE SALES AND COSTS			
SALES					
Drink	62,039.80	51,339.40	7,364.95	3,335.45	
Bottle	18,687.25	5,725.50	12,961.75		
Total Sales	80,727.05	57,064.90	20,326.70	3,335.45	
Potential	81,198.75	57,578.10	20,223.55	3,397.10	
Bar Difference (over or short)	471.70	513.20	103.15	61.65	
Per Cent of Difference	.6	.9	.5	1.8	
COST OF SALES					
Drink	19,229.88	16,052.02	2,147.54	1,030.32	
Bottle	8,642.04	2,711.87	5,930.17		
Total	27,871.92	18,763.89	8,077.71	1,030.32	
PERCENTAGE COST					
Drink	30.9	31.3	29.2	30.9	
Bottle	46.2	47.4	45.7		
Actual	34.5	32.9	39.7	30.9	
Potential	34.3	32.6	39.9	30.3	
Difference	.2	.3	.2	.6	

FIGURE 29. *Analysis of beverage sales and costs.*

30B will give you some idea of the purposes for which the tests are made. Testing is done regularly to ensure that the yield is the same or to attempt to find a better yield; these tests are usually made on uncooked food that is purchased in bulk and then cut up into various pieces. Portion tests are made on both cooked and uncooked foods, not only to determine portion sizes but also to find out the quality of the food, since it is not the practice to substitute a larger portion of poor food for a smaller portion of good food.

By now it should be apparent that the duties of the food controller encompass the complete food and beverage operation, and it should also be apparent that this position is a very fine one in which to obtain experience and overall hotel knowledge.

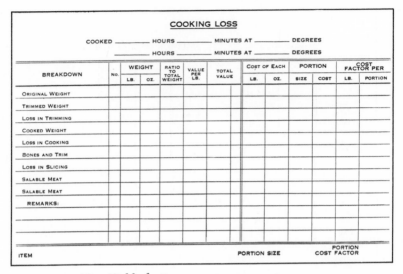

FIGURE 30A. *Yield chart.*

COORDINATION WITH OTHER DEPARTMENTS

In the catering department it is necessary to have a liaison man who will work with top management, with all other departments in the hotel, and within the catering department itself. The title of this person may differ from hotel to hotel; here he will be referred to as the catering manager.

The catering manager is assistant to the general manager of the hotel and is responsible to him for the operation of the catering department. His main duties are to see that management's policies are carried out and that his department makes the desired profit. To perform these wide duties, the catering manager must concern himself with minute details. He must cooperate with all department heads, watch food and beverage costs, control payroll, and decide when overtime is necessary. He must decide when to purchase regular equipment and whether other items are needed. He must decide when prices are to be raised and whether a change in the menu will help or hurt business.

The catering manager must attend various meetings such as those held by the antibreakage committee and the safety committee, since his department is directly affected. He must be present when the sales manager is trying to book gatherings that will have food or beverage served. He must make suggestions and carry out new ideas to help business. He must talk to salesmen about new products that may cut costs and increase business. He must watch the inventories of food, beverages, china, glass, and silver to be sure that they are not so large that they are tying up hotel money which should be bearing interest. He must check all the public restaurants, banquet rooms, ballrooms, and kitchens daily to see that food and service are up to standards. He must hold food meetings several times a week to discuss any problems that may arise. The catering manager must necessarily attend to many little things, but his main concern is to see that everyone in his department is doing his job and that the entire operation runs smoothly.

FIGURE 30B. *Butcher test card.*

BUTCHER TEST CARD												
ITEM __Strip Loin__ GRADE __Prime__ DATE __8/23/—__												
PIECES __2__ WEIGHING __47__ LBS __4__ OZ. AVERAGE WEIGHT __23-10__												
TOTAL COST $ __69.93__ AT $ __1.48__ PER __1b.__ SUPPLIER __Ottman__ HOTEL												
BREAKDOWN	NO.	WEIGHT		RATIO TO TOTAL WEIGHT	VALUE PER LB.	TOTAL VALUE		COST OF EACH		PORTION		COST FACTOR PER	
		LB.	OZ.					LB.	OZ.	SIZE	COST	LB.	PORTION
Sirloin Steak	13	11	12	24.9	269	31	61	269	168	14oz	235	1.82	1.59
Minute Steak	18	12	11	26.9	269	34	13	269	168	11oz	185	1.82	1.25
Club Steak (snd)	1		7	.9	269	1	18	269	168	7oz	118	1.82	.79
Hamburger		4	10	9.8	65	3	1	65	41	8oz	325	.44	.22
Waste		15	12	33.3									
Shrinkage		2		4.2									
TOTAL		47	4	100%	148	69	93						
ITEM PORTION SIZE PORTION COST FACTOR													

CHAPTER 5

Personnel and Accounting

Transforming the specialized skills and performances of the departments discussed in the preceding chapters into a smooth flowing hotel operation requires tremendous skill in human relations. Most businesses have established a department to assist management in this vital function. This department—personnel—has the specialized duty of selecting, servicing, and improving the human team.

Just as it would be impossible to operate a hotel without people, a business would be chaos without accounting. Accounting is the language of business, and it holds a position of prime importance in the hotel industry. Both the personnel and accounting functions are staff by nature, but both are indispensable to successful hotel operation.

THE PERSONNEL DEPARTMENT

A glance at the organizations charts of our small, medium, and large hotels (Figures 1, 2, and 3) will reveal that only in the large operation is even one person specifically assigned the duties of personnel management. The hotel industry typifies the old paradox, "They who need a service the most, use it the least." Here is an industry whose very lifeblood is the human element we have discussed, but one that fails to spend even a portion of the time, money, or care for the human resource that it regularly provides for the electrical and mechanical equipment of the hotel.

Because my background and training have been in personnel management, I have often been asked why hotels place so little emphasis on personnel. This is a difficult question to answer, and the reasons I *have* been able to discern do not provide a definitive answer. Many hotelmen feel that their industry has numerous unique aspects which will not permit the adoption of personnel techniques and practices that are in everyday use in other industries. There are also those men who resist personnel ideas simply because they are new to the industry. This latter group, of course, resists change of any type, but fortunately it represents a small minority. Other executives are suspicious of any personnel philosophy because to them it appears to be mollycoddling and represents a philosophy opposed to the one they have successfully followed for years. When one considers the inroads recently made by labor unions in the hotel business, this attitude can readily be understood.

These facts may be somewhat misleading. Personnel direction is a vital function of management—a thread that runs through the whole cloth. The function itself must be performed to some degree or management could not exist. The absence of a position specifically labeled personnel director does not necessarily mean that the function is not being performed. We saw in Chapter 2 that the majority of hotels in this country contain 100 rooms or less. An organization of this size cannot ordinarily afford a full-time personnel director.

While personnel management may have been understated in the past, it has now come into its own and is very much in the spotlight throughout the hotel industry. Two factors have contributed to this development. First, the trend to chain operation has swallowed up many of the independent hotels, and a chain operation can well afford personnel specialists because the cost can be distributed across many hotels. Second, the principal management problems of today's hotel world center around the employees and the personnel function.

Recruitment, Selection, and Placement

Over the years the hotel industry has had difficulty in attracting the type of people needed in sufficient numbers. It is generally believed that the major portion of the labor market is unaware or at least poorly informed about the nature of hotel work and the diversity of occupational skills needed. The personnel director must overcome this obstacle because he is charged with recruiting employees at all levels of skill as they are needed. He must know his local labor market and be able to design a program that will attract large numbers of qualified employees to his hotel. When the labor market is tight, this job becomes a genuine challenge.

If he succeeds in his recruitment task, he now has several applicants for each opening and he now faces problem number two—which of the applicants are best qualified, which will be good workers, and which will be stable, long-service employees. He must, in other words, operate a selection program. The final selection may rest with the department head, but personnel must screen each applicant and provide the department head with pertinent data upon which to make his selection. Detailed knowledge of interviewing, job requirements, tests and measurements of human abilities, and other skills are a must for the personnel man.

Placement is primarily matching people with jobs. The better the selection devices and the job descriptions and specifications, the easier becomes the task of placing the right person in the right job. It should be pointed out that supervising the writing of job descriptions and the development of job specifications is another duty of the personnel office.

Hotels generally have a high turnover rate and this in turn magnifies the recruitment problem. To reduce turnover is a prime objective of the personnel department. It is conservatively estimated that every time a worker must be replaced, the hotel loses a minimum of $100 in direct and indirect costs. One method of reducing turnover is through an effective induction or orientation program. Responsibility for the design of such a program rests with personnel.

Productivity

The profit squeeze has been on for some time. To increase income has been difficult and to keep costs from rising has been impossible. In searching for methods to increase profit potential, the hotel industry has focused on employee productivity. In the past year every major conference, convention, and seminar has included discussions on productivity.

Many comparisons have been made, but one or two will suffice for our purposes. It is estimated that general industry is about 80 percent efficient today. The best estimates available on the hotel industry show it at 45 percent efficiency. Such a comparison, however, is unfair because of a number of factors. The author is not suggesting that hotels can or should be at 80 percent. However, there is general agreement that hotels must increase productivity if they are to stay in business. One study reveals that between the years 1959 and 1965, productivity actually decreased slightly. Such figures do not make owners and managers sleep well.

A great deal of time, thought, and effort is being expended to hatch ideas for improving the productivity factor. Perhaps the greatest potential is within the employees themselves. To achieve this potential, the employees must be motivated! Who is our expert on motivation? Again, the logical man is our personnel expert. He is the reservoir of human relations knowledge upon which all members of management must draw in order to meet the challenge.

Other Responsibilities

Wages and salaries are a vital part of any business organization. There is a continuous need to check wages against the community levels and to be sure they are competitive in the labor market. The personnel director must conduct job evaluation studies and wage surveys. Closely associated with wages are the fringe benefits and incentive systems. Management looks to personnel for advice, suggestions, and the latest developments in these areas. The personnel director must be well informed.

One of the department's greatest responsibilities is training. Experienced workers with the skills needed for hotel work are getting scarcer every day. The only way to develop a competent staff today is to train it. The personnel director cannot do all the training; supervisors, department heads and executives must accept this responsibility. The techniques of training must be supplied to these people by the personnel director. Training will be at every level from semi-skilled to supervisory development.

Promotion pathways must be charted and explained to the employees. Promotables should be identified, merit rating systems devised and instituted. All sorts of personnel records must be constantly updated.

Then there is the number one problem of all business—communication. The personnel director is constantly seeking ways to keep the communication channels open and functioning. It is his duty to keep misconceptions, erroneous rumors, and misunderstandings at a minimum. A very important function is to create a grievance system that is effective.

He must never be too busy to discuss a problem with an employee. He is chaplain, psychiatrist, and sociologist all at the same time. His role is to be the architect of company morale and the catalyst that unites all elements of the hotel into a smoothly functioning machine whose objective is to provide the very best service possible.

THE ACCOUNTING DEPARTMENT

You should understand that most functions of the accounting department are of a technical nature, and they require a good deal of background and training for complete comprehension. Of necessity, therefore, certain parts of this section must be oversimplified in order to provide a clear picture of departmental duties and procedures. The importance of accounting in the hotel business cannot be overemphasized. Every manager should have a knowledge of and a background in accounting procedures. You should realize, however, that all accounting is a means to an end and not an end in itself.

The work of the accounting department, supervised by the auditor, falls into four categories: revenue, expenses, payroll, and statistical reports. (As an example of such reports, see Figure 31, a portion of a staffing schedule.) Perhaps the best way to begin a description of revenue is to consider a guest using the hotel's services and charging them to his account.

Revenue

Figures 32 and 33 illustrate two charges (valet and dinner) made by a Mr. Jones. These forms are sent from the department

STEWARD

Normal Volume Range of Total Weekly Food Covers

Job Classification or Group	Hours in Work Week	Upper Limit	10,000 Employees		9,600 Employees		9,200 Employees		Lower Limit
			On Staff	On Duty	On Staff	On Duty	On Staff	On Duty	
Warewashers	40		21.2	15.1	20.2	14.5	19.2	13.7	
All Other									
Kitchen Cleaners	40		2.0	1.4	2.0	1.4	2.0	1.4	
Potwashers	40		3.0	2.1	3.0	2.1	3.0	2.1	
Food Runners	40		1.7	1.2	1.5	1.0	1.5	1.0	
Icemen	40		1.5	1.0	1.5	1.0	1.5	1.0	
Yardmen	40		2.4	2.1	2.4	2.1	2.4	2.1	
Silver Burnisher	40		1.0	.7	1.0	.7	1.0	.7	
Kitchen Stewards	40		3.0	2.1	3.0	2.1	3.0	2.1	
Total All Other			14.6	10.6	14.4	10.4	14.4	10.4	
TOTAL STEWARDS			35.8	25.7	34.6	24.9	33.6	24.1	

FIGURE 31. *Staffing guide.*

concerned to the front office cashier, who posts the charges to Mr. Jones's folio. A typical folio set is shown in Figure 34 (the guest's copy) and Figure 35 (the hotel's copy). All charges coming to the front office cashier must be posted in either the guest ledger or the city ledger. The guest ledger contains all accounts of people staying in the hotel, and the city ledger contains accounts of local businessmen and credit-card accounts of people

FIGURE 32. *Valet check. (Courtesy Brown Palace Hotel.)*

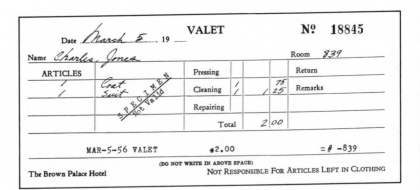

not residing in the hotel. If a guest checks out and requests the hotel to send him the bill, his account will be transferred from the guest ledger to the city ledger.

In former days the posting of charges to accounts was done by hand. Today, machines accomplish this work in a matter of a few minutes, and practically every hotel front office has National Cash Register units for this purpose. The larger the hotel, the greater the number of machines required for efficient operation. Our example hotel uses two machines, one for the guest ledger and one for the city ledger.

At the close of each day's business a complete recap of the type and amount of business done, department by department, is needed. The man who compiles this report is the night auditor. His sources of information are cashier reports from each department producing revenue, the city ledger N.C.R. machine, and the guest ledger N.C.R. machine.

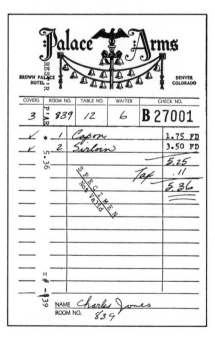

FIGURE 33. *Dinner check. (Courtesy Brown Palace Hotel.)*

JONES, CHARLES		839					100002
ANYTOWN, USA		1/9.00			DENVER		
3/4/19--	3.30 PM						
MEMO.		DATE	EXPLANATION		CHARGES	CREDITS	BAL. DUE
	1	MAR-4	REST'R -	TAV	* 6.24		
	2	MAR-4	-Pd Out	TIP	* 0.75		
	3	MAR-4	ROOM -		* 9.00		
	4	MAR-4	PHONE -		* 0.60		* 16.59
	5	MAR-5	VALET -		* 2.00		
	6	MAR-5	REST'R -	P'AR	* 5.36		* 23.95
	7	MAR-5	-PAID			*23.95	* 0.00
	8						
	9						
	10						
	11						
	12						
	13						
	14						
	15						
	16						
	17						
	18						
	19						
	20						
	21						
	22						
	23						
	24						

WE HAVE TRIED TO MAKE YOUR STAY AT THE BROWN PALACE
A PLEASANT AND ENJOYABLE ONE.

WHEN YOU NEXT COME TO DENVER, PLEASE ADVISE US IN AD-
VANCE THE TYPE OF ACCOMMODATIONS YOU PREFER, AS WE ARE
ANXIOUS TO PROVIDE THE PARTICULAR TYPE OF ROOM WHICH
YOU DESIRE. A CHEERFUL WELCOME WILL BE AWAITING YOU.

A — BARBER SHOP   E — TICKETS
B — BEAUTY SHOP   F — FLORIST
C — CASH ADVANCE   G — GARAGE
D — BAGGAGE   H — MEETING ROOM
V — MEDICAL

1629

LAST BALANCE IS AMOUNT DUE
UNLESS OTHERWISE INDICATED
BILLS ARE PAYABLE WHEN PRESENTED

FIGURE 34. *Guest's folio—guest copy.*
(Courtesy Brown Palace Hotel.)

The night auditor starts with his food and beverage recap, using a form similar to the one shown in Figure 36. Working from the cashier's reports, he fills in all of the columns and arrives at figures for total sales under each of the column headings. He checks the registers, and the total food sales and total beverage sales indicated must agree with the totals shown. Notice that in Figure 36 total sales of food and total sales of beverages and liquors do agree with the total figure at the bottom of the page under these columns. If there is a discrepancy, the night auditor must find the error and take action to correct it. If the error is in

MEMO.		DATE	EXPLANATION	CHARGES	CREDITS	BAL. DUE	PICK-UP	ROOM NO.

JONES, CHARLES   839
ANYTOWN, USA
       1/9.00
3/4/19--   3.30 PM

FROM FOLIO
TO FOLIO

DENVER

100001

	MONDAY	TUESDAY	WEDNESDAY	THURSDAY	FRIDAY	SATURDAY	SUNDAY	CHANGED		
								DATE	TO ROOM	NEW RATE
LOCAL PHONE CALLS										

MEMO.		DATE	EXPLANATION	CHARGES	CREDITS	BAL. DUE	PICK-UP	ROOM NO.
	1	MAR-4	REST'R - TAV	* 6.24				=#-8.39
	2	MAR-4	-Pd Out TIP	* 0.75				=#-8.39
	3	MAR-4	ROOM -	* 9.00				=#-8.39
	4	MAR-4	PHONE -	* 0.60		* 16.59	* 16.59	=#-8.39
	5	MAR-5	VALET -	* 2.00				=#-8.39
	6	MAR-5	REST'R - P'AR	* 5.36		* 23.95	* 23.95	=#-8.39
	7	MAR-5	-PAID		* 23.95	* 0.00		=#-8.39
	8							
	9							
	10							
	11							
	12							
	13							
	14							
	15							
	16							
	17							
	18							
	19							
	20							
	21							
	22							
	23							
	24							

SPECIMEN Not Valid

REMARKS

TRANSFER TO CITY LEDGER   1629

GUEST'S SIGNATURE _____

CHARGE TO _____

ADDRESS _____

APPROVED BY _____

Press of The National Cash Register Co., Dayton, Ohio

FIGURE 35. *Guest's folio—hotel copy.*
(Courtesy Brown Palace Hotel.)

his own computation, it can readily be corrected. Other errors may range from minor to serious and may be accidental mistakes or attempts on the part of some employee to defraud the hotel. Whatever the error, it must be located and explained. Figure 37 shows a portion of a cashier's report with which the night auditor works. At this point he has a complete recap of the day's revenue in the food department and the beverage department.

BROWN PALACE HOTEL

FOOD AND BEVERAGE RECAP. DATE *March 5, 19 —*

	NUMBER COVERS	CASH SALES	GUEST LEDGER	CITY LEDGER	TOTAL SALES	FOOD	BEVERAGES AND LIQUORS	COVER CHARGES	SALES TAX	FED. TAX
PALACE ARMS										
LUNCH	99	173.61	23.10	59.36	256.07	192.40	59.75		3.92	
DINNER	122	366.63	56.94	100.52	524.09	448.70	66.35		9.04	
TOTAL	221	540.24	80.04	159.88	780.16	641.10	126.10		12.96	
EMERALD ROOM										
LUNCH	104	155.51	2.49	70.50	228.50	189.20	35.50		3.80	
DINNER	73	244.39	81.61	10.92	336.92	236.15	47.90	6.00	4.76	42.11
ALIBI BAR		108.30	8.15	16.55	133.00		126.60			6.40
TOTAL	177	508.20	92.25	97.97	698.42	425.35	210.00	6.00	8.56	48.51
SHIP TAVERN										
LUNCH	186	264.77	54.47	165.41	484.65	242.55	236.75		5.35	
DINNER	159	532.86	77.11	169.69	779.66	365.30	406.85		7.51	
BAR SALES		177.25			177.25		177.25			
TOTAL	345	974.88	131.58	335.10	1441.56	607.85	820.85		12.86	
COFFEE TERRACE										
BREAKFAST	347	265.72	97.78	18.92	382.42	374.60			7.82	
LUNCH	191	205.89	19.55	39.08	264.52	250.10	9.25		5.17	
TOTAL	538	471.61	117.33	58.00	646.94	624.70	9.25		12.99	
ROOM SERVICE										
BREAKFAST	89	15.11	128.98		144.09	120.70		20.50	2.89	
LUNCH	32	4.28	60.16	2.29	66.73	59.20	5.10	1.20	1.23	
DINNER	34	17.61	122.99	.60	141.20	78.45	47.40	13.25	2.10	
TOTAL	155	37.00	312.13	2.89	352.02	258.35	52.50	34.95	6.22	
BANQUETS										
BREAKFAST										
LUNCH	43			123.80	123.80	90.00	32.00		1.80	
DINNER	120	25.50		732.75	758.25	500.00	248.25		10.00	
TOTAL	163	25.50		856.55	882.05	590.00	280.25		11.80	
WINE STEWARD		4.00	9.00	2.75	15.75		15.50			.25
TOTAL SALES	1599	2561.43	742.33	1513.14	4816.90	3147.35	1514.45	40.95	65.39	48.76
CHECKING REG.										
PALACE ARMS						641.10				
TAVERN A							202.70			
TAVERN D						595.35	744.60			
ALIBI BAR							541.00			
SERVICE BAR							28.55			
KITCHEN						2033.25				
COMPS.						(78.85)	(2.40)			
COVER CHARGES						(40.95)				
VOIDS						(2.55)				
TOTAL						3147.35	1514.45			

FIGURE 36. *Food and beverage recap.*
(Courtesy Brown Palace Hotel.)

The night auditor's next step is to complete the rooms revenue. He posts all room charges to the guest accounts, working in conjunction with the night clerk, who is preparing his

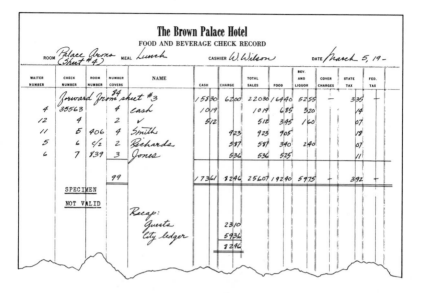

FIGURE 37. *Food and beverage check record. (Courtesy Brown Palace Hotel.)*

report. As stated earlier, the two reports must agree on individual room charges and total room revenue. The night auditor also posts any late charges that might have come in after the front office cashier leaves at 11 P.M. Once all rooms and late charges are posted, the night auditor gets his machine totals for each of the first seventeen categories shown on Figure 30—the night auditor's machine balance. Having obtained his machine totals, he must then compare these totals with the totals he has received on the individual department reports. For example, the valet sales report in Figure 39 shows guest charges of $95.45, which agrees with the guest-ledger machine total. If you look again at Figure 38 you will see that each of the machine totals checks with the net totals. If there were a discrepancy, it would be checked and re-checked until the error was located and corrected. Such an investigation would be carried out by means of the N.C.R. auditing machine strip shown in Figure 40.

SPECIMEN

NOT VALID

D—NIGHT AUDITOR'S MACHINE BALANCE No. _2 (guests)_

○

DATE _March 5_ ___ 19___

MEMO.		DATE	DEPARTMENT	NET TOTALS	CORRECTIONS	MACH. TOTALS	NUMBER OF ITEMS
MISCELLANEOUS	1	MAR-5	MISC. —	336.15		* 336.15	=# -
LAUNDRY	2	MAR-5	L'NDRY —	77.27		* 77.27	=# -
VALET	3	MAR-5	VALET —	95.45		* 95.45	=# -
RESTAURANT	4	MAR-5	REST'R —	742.33		* 742.33	=# -
LOCAL PHONE	5	MAR-5	PHONE —	68.40		* 68.40	=# -
ROOM	6	MAR-5	ROOM —	3495.30	(8.00)	*3,503.30	=# -
LONG DISTANCE	7	MAR-5	L'DIST —	232.40		* 232.40	=# -
TRANS. FROM CHG. ACCT.	8	MAR-5	FR'LED —	—		* 0.00	=# -
TRANS. DEBIT FORWARD	9	MAR-5	F'WARD —	—		* 0.00	=# -
NEWS	10	MAR-5	—NEWS	4.25		* 4.25	=# -
PORTER	11	MAR-5	—PORT'R	12.50		* 12.50	=# -
TELEGRAM	12	MAR-5	—TELG'M	18.47		* 18.47	=# -
PAID OUT	13	MAR-5	—Pd Out	222.59		* 222.59	=# -
TOTAL DEBITS	14			5305.11			
PAID	15	MAR-5	—PAID	4245.04		*4,245.04	=# -
ADJUSTMENT	16	MAR-5	—R'BATE	7.65		* 7.65	=# -
TRANS. TO CHG. ACCT.	17	MAR-5	—TO'LED	1510.75		*1,510.75	=# -
TRANS. CREDIT FORWARD	18	MAR-5	—F'WARD			* 0.00	=# -
TOTAL CREDITS	19			5763.44			
NET DEBITS	20			(458.33) CR.			
OPENING DR. BALANCE	21			4479.09			
TOTAL MACHINE DR. BAL.	22					5,765.95	
LESS MACHINE CR. BAL.	23					(1,745.19)	
NET OUTSTANDING	24			4,020.76		4,020.76	

PRINTED U.S.A. B-913—D24SS—PRESS OF THE NATIONAL CASH REGISTER CO., DAYTON, OHIO   PRINTERS 661-662

AFTER CLEARING MACHINE AS ABOVE, SEE THAT THE FOLLOWING ARE DONE. (CHECK EACH AS DONE.)
1. DATE WHEELS ARE CHANGED.
2. ROWS 2 AND 3 ARE CLEARED ON NEW AUDIT STRIP.
   (I. E. REGISTER ALL KEYS TO SHOW ZERO.)
3. ITEM COUNTERS ARE SET AT ZERO.
4. LOWER LOCK OF ROW 1 IS LOCKED.
5. THERE IS SUFFICIENT AUDIT STRIP.

FIGURE 38. _Night auditor's machine balance._

The first thirteen items on the night auditor's machine balance (Figure 38) are debits, which means that guest accounts have been charged with these figures. Items fifteen through eighteen are credits, which means guest accounts have been crdited with these amounts. The paid category is cash received from departing guests in settlement of their accounts. When the credits equal the debits on an individual account, there is no

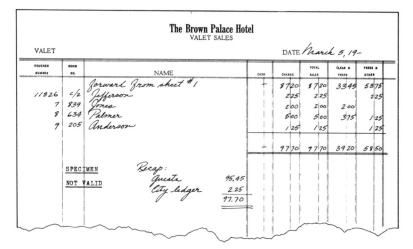

FIGURE 39. *Valet sales report. (Courtesy Brown Palace Hotel.)*

balance. In Figure 34, when Mr. Jones paid his bill, the amount appeared as a credit to his account. The paid out category consists of tips written on signed checks and cash advances to the guest which are charged to his account. Category seventeen contains accounts transferred from the guest ledger to the city ledger.

For this particular day, total credits exceeded total debits, so there is a credit balance to apply to the accounts receivable. Accounts receivable is revenue earned by the hotel for which it has not yet received payment. The opening balance for the day is the exact amount of the accounts receivable at that time. If the day's transactions result in a debit balance, this amount (total debits minus total credits) is added to the opening balance. If credits exceed debits, the credit balance is subtracted from the opening balance. The figure in either case is the closing balance, and it becomes the opening balance for the following day. In Figure 38 the opening balance of $14,479.09 was reduced by the

```
MISC. —              *  0.00 S       B • •
L'NDRY —             *  0.00 S       B • •
VALET —              *  0.00 S       B • •
RESTR —              *  0.00 S       B • •
PHONE —              *  0.00 S       B • •
ROOM —               *  0.00 S       B • •
L'DIST —             *  0.00 S       B • •
CHGA/C —             *  0.00 S       B • •
F'WARD —             *  0.00 S       B • •
   — TRIAL           *  0.00 S S     B • •
   — NEWS            *  0.00 S       B • •
   — PORT'R          *  0.00 S       B • •
   — TEL C'H         *  0.00 S       B • •
   — Pd Out          *  0.00 S       B • •
   — PAID            *  0.00 S       B • •
   — ADJ'ST          *  0.00 S       B • •
   — CHGA/C          *  0.00 S       B • •
   — F'WARD          *  0.00 S       B • •
   --                     *  0.00 F  B • •
RESTR —      D*  2.06                 B •333
   --                *  2.06 •        B •333
   --                     *  0.00 F   B • •
RESTR —      C*  1.30                 B •434
   — Pd Out  S*  0.25                 B •434
   --                *  1.55 •        B •434
   --                     *  10.90 F  B •607
L'DIST —     S*  2.24                 B •607
   --                *  13.14 •       B •607
   --                     *  13.14 F  B •607
   — PAID        S*  13.14            B •607
   --                *  0.00 •        B •607
   --                     *  16.59 F  B •839
VALET —      S*  2.00                 B •839
RESTR —      K*  5.36                 B •839
   --                *  23.95 •       B •839
   --                     *  10.00 G  B •222
L'NDRY —     $*  2.23                 B •222
   --                *  7.77 G*       B •222
   --                                 
```

FIGURE 40. *Auditing machine strip.*

day's credit balance of $458.33, giving a closing balance of $14,020.76.

The night auditor follows exactly the same procedure with

the city ledger N.C.R. machine. He now has compiled and audited the day's revenue from each department of the hotel. He turns over to the auditor the food and beverage recap, the

FIGURE 41. *Daily revenue report. (Courtesy Brown Palace Hotel.)*

BROWN PALACE HOTEL

DAILY REVENUE REPORT

DATE *March 5, 19–*

	CASH SALES	GUEST LEDGER	CITY LEDGER	GROSS REVENUE	FEDERAL TAX	SALES TAX	GENERAL LEDGER	NET REVENUE
ROOMS—Transient		3416 30		3416 30				3416 30
Permanent		79 00		79 00				79 00
TOTAL ROOMS		3495 30		3495 30				3495 30
FOOD AND BEVERAGES	2561 43	742 33	1513 14	4816 90	48 76	65 39		4702 75
TELEPHONE—Local		68 40	3 60	72 00				72 00
Long Distance		232 40	1 76	234 16				234 16
Booth Com.								
TOTAL TELEPHONE		300 80	5 36	306 16				306 16
BARBER SHOP	148 00			148 00				148 00
BEAUTY SALON	65 25			65 25				65 25
VALET		95 45	2 25	97 70				97 70
GUEST LAUNDRY		77 27	13 22	90 49				90 49
FLOWER SHOP	50 83	5 15	90 25	146 23		3 11		143 12
CHECK ROOMS	13 00			13 00				13 00
Concessions			33 65	33 65				33 65
Radio Rental		15 00		15 00				15 00
Coin Locks								
Grease Sales		36 00		36 00				36 00
Vending Machines						SPECIMEN		
Breakage								
Salvage Sales						NOT VALID		
Other Income		15 00	100 00	115 00				115 00
TOTAL MINOR DEPT.		66 00	133 65	199 65				199 65
STORE RENTALS			66 13	66 13				66 13
STEWARD SALES—Food								
Liquors								
GENERAL LEDGER *#211*		265 00		265 00			265 00	
OVER AND SHORT	95			95				95
TOTAL REVENUE	2839 46	5047 30	1824 00	9710 76	48 76	68 50	265 00	9328 50
CASH PAID OUT		257 81	73 81	331 62				
TOTAL CHARGES	2839 46	5305 11	1897 81	10042 38				

CASH RECEIPTS			ACCOUNTS RECEIVABLE	GUESTS	CITY	TOTAL
CASH SALES		2839 46				
GUESTS LEDGER	4245 04		OPENING BALANCE	14479 09	72422 13	86901 22
CITY LEDGER	4784 88		CHARGES	5305 11	1897 81	7202 92
ACCTS. REC. COLL.		9029 92	TRANSFERS	(1510 75)	1510 75	—
GROSS CASH		11869 38	CASH COLLECTED	(4245 04)	(4784 88)	(9029 92)
LESS—PAID OUT		(331 62)	REBATES	(7 65)	—	(7 65)
NET DEPOSIT		11537 76	CLOSING BALANCE	14020 76	71045 81	85066 57

guest-ledger machine balance, and the city-ledger machine balance with all supporting figures and forms.

Working with the figures provided by the night auditor, the auditor draws up a daily revenue report such as that shown in Figure 41. By looking through the other forms in this section, you can trace the origin of most of the figures on this report. The net

FIGURE 42A. *Daily report (front).*

DAILY REPORT THE				HOTEL			
WEATHER_____ DAY_____				DATE_____			19__
	CHARGE	CASH	TODAY	THIS MONTH	LAST MONTH	'LAST YEAR	
Rooms							
Food-Beverages							
Cover Charges							
Telephone							
Barber Shop							
Beauty Salon							
Valet							
Guest Laundry							
Flower Shop							
Misc. Incomes							
Total Revenue							
Federal Tax							
Sales Tax							
Total							
Add: Accts. Rec. Collected							
Total Deposit							

ROOM STATISTICS:	TODAY	TOTAL TO DATE		
		THIS MONTH	LAST MONTH	LAST YEAR
Room Earnings				
Per cent of Occupancy				
Number of Rooms Occupied				
Number of Guests				
Average Rate per Occupied Room				
Average Rate per Guest				

FOOD SALES:	PERSONS TO DATE						
	This Mo.	Last Mo.	Last Year				
Palace Arms							
Emerald Room							
Ship Tavern							
Coffee Terrace							
Room Service							
Banquets							
TOTAL FOOD SALES							
BEVERAGE SALES							
Palace Arms							
Alibi Bar							
Ship Tavern							
Coffee Terrace							
Room Service							
Banquets							
Wine Steward							
TOTAL BEVERAGE SALES							
RECAP: Rooms							
Food							
Beverages							
TOTAL ROOMS, FOOD AND BEVERAGES							

BANK BALANCES	SPECIAL ACCOUNT	GENERAL ACCOUNT	PROOF OF ACCOUNTS RECEIVABLE	
Balance Brought Forward			Balance Forward	
Add: Today's Deposit			Add: Today's Total Rev.	
Total			Total	
Deduct Today's Withdrawals			Deduct: Today's Cash	
			Total	
Balance in Bank			Deduct: Today's Allowances	
		Auditor	Balance Accts. Receivable	

revenue figures are of primary importance. Notice the recap of cash receipts and accounts receivable at the bottom of Figure 41. We have accounted for all charges in the hotel for the day and the cash received in payment of accounts in the city and guest ledgers, all of which pass through the front office cashier. This leaves only the receipts from cash sales in the various departments to be covered. Each cashier has her own bank for which she has signed in the auditor's office. During her shift she records

FIGURE 42B. *Daily report (back).*

DAILY REPORT THE _____ HOTEL						
ROOM STATISTICS						
	REVENUE	NO. ROOMS	NO. GUESTS	AVERAGE PER ROOM	AVERAGE PER GUEST	% OCCUPIED
Transients						
Permanents						
TOTAL						

	TODAY	TO DATE	LAST MONTH	LAST YEAR
Rooms—Transient				
Permanent				
Skyline—Transient				
Permanent				
TOTAL				

	THIS MONTH	TO DATE LAST MONTH	LAST YEAR
Number of Employees Today			
Average Meal Check			
Average Banquet Check			

MISC. INCOME

MONTH OF	%		THIS MONTH	
		Check Rooms		
		Concessions		
		Radio Rentals		
		Coin Locks		
Occupancy		Breakage		
Wages to Rev. Rooms		Grease Sales		
Wages to Rev. Food		Store Rentals		
Wages to Rev. Total		Salvage Sales		
Food		Other Income		
Beverage		Steward Sale (Food)		
		Steward Sale (Liquor)		
		Vending Machines		
		Over and Short		
		TOTAL		

all transactions, whether cash or charge. She accepts all cash payments, and when she completes her shift all cash in excess of her regular bank is placed in an envelope which goes to the general cashier. She checks her bank into a safe provided by the hotel. The next morning the general cashier counts all cash receipts, compares the totals with the revenue report recap, and makes up the daily deposit.

Having compiled, checked, and certified all revenue data from the previous day, the auditor then makes up the daily report, which goes directly to the manager to inform him of the day's activities. The daily report is a vital tool for the manager, as it provides him with a complete picture of the operation, is a

FIGURE 43.   *Invoice.*

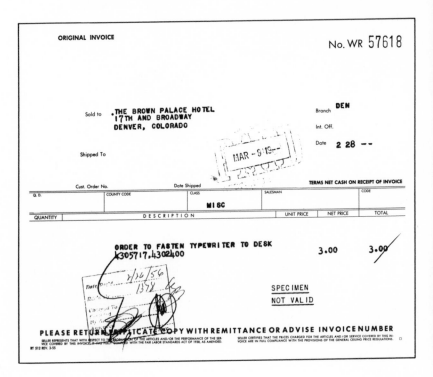

guide to what actions he should take, and indicates any weak spots. You can be sure that information from this report will furnish data for discussion with department heads and other members of the staff. A sample daily report is shown in Figures 42A and 42B, although there is no standard form for this. Each manager has his own ideas as to what information he needs and wants, and determines the data the auditor will provide in the daily report.

With the morning reports out of the way, the accounting department turns its attention to recording the revenue figures in the books. The net revenue figures for each department, taken from the daily revenue report, are posted in the sales journal. At the end of the month the departmental totals of the sales journal are posted to the ledger. The remaining step is to transfer figures from the ledger to the monthly financial statements. (These statements are discussed at the end of this section.)

Notice that all checks, registration cards, and folios carry serial numbers, which are for control or protection purposes. Each of these forms is checked in the accounting office to make sure that all of them are accounted for. Should one or more be missing, an immediate investigation starts.

Expenses

The second category of accounting work involves the handling of expenses. All purchases by the hotel must be certified, recorded, and paid. Large hotels have a purchasing agent, and all purchases are made through his office; however, because the majority of hotels are not large enough to necessitate such a position, I have not included it in this treatment.

Purchases are made by individual department heads, with the approval of the manager. In most cases the manager's approval is merely a formality, since the goods have already arrived and may be in use. I do not mean to imply that the manager has no control over purchases. The manager knows his department heads and their integrity, and in case of any large expenditures the department head will always consult the manager and obtain his approval before entering an order for the items involved. In hotels using a purchase order system, the manager, in reality, approves every expenditure before it is made. A purchase order

FIGURE 44. *Purchase voucher. (Coutresy Brown Palace Hotel.)*

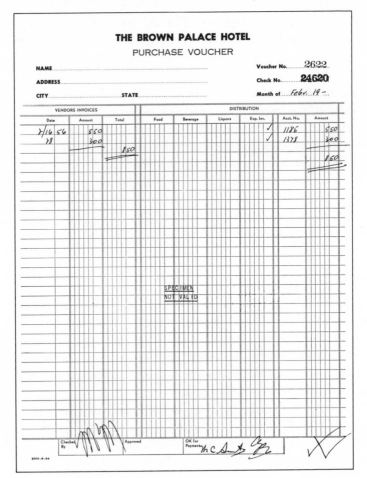

system provides close control over expenses but it also involves much more paperwork than other systems. Which system is used depends entirely on the management policy of each individual hotel.

Now let us follow a simple purchase through the accounting channels. A department head places an order, and an invoice such as that shown in Figure 43 arrives in the accounting office. It is stamped as being received, and then sent to the department head involved. He will initial the invoice to signify that the *goods* have been received, that they are in order, and that the charge is correct. The invoice is then returned to the accounts payable clerk, who posts the invoice to the purchase voucher shown in Figure 44. The clerk checks additions and extensions and routes the invoice to the auditor, who charges the purchase to the appropriate expense account. In Figure 44 the purchase is charged to account 1185, which is the expense inventory of the department ordering the goods. From here the invoice is sent to the manager for approval, then returned to the accounts payable clerk who distributes the figures; i.e., she checks the proper category and lists the account number and the amount of the purchase. At the end of the month she totals the amounts, figures in any allowable discount, and sends the voucher to the auditor. He writes a check for the correct amount, which is sent to the purveyor. The voucher is entered in the voucher register and the check in the check register. The check and voucher registers are closed to the ledger. At the end of the month, the ledgers are totaled and the financial statements are prepared.

For food and beverage, the above procedure is altered somewhat. The invoice arrives with the food or beverage. The steward and his receiving clerk check all foods and beverages for quantity, quality, and price before accepting them. The steward stamps the invoice and certifies it all in one step. He forwards the invoice to the accounting office, who performs the necessary charges, distributions, and postings.

Salaries and Wages

The third principal area of work in accounting involves the preparation and payment of salaries and wages. In the hotel industry it is almost universal practice to pay twice monthly. The payroll periods usually run from the first to the fifteenth and from the sixteenth to the thirtieth of the month, and employees are paid on the fifth and twentieth of the month.

The payroll clerk sets up an individual earnings record and fills out a time card for every employee. The usual federal tax forms must be filed, and notation of any deductions for insurance, bonds, or charities, must be made. During the payroll period, the clerk makes up the payroll recap sheet, which lists all employees by departments. On the fifteenth of the month the time cards are pulled and compared with the time books kept by department heads. The clerk computes the gross pay for each employee and enters these figures in the time book. At this point all deductions must be computed and recorded and the net pay figure arrived at for each employee. This information must appear on the check stubs, the individual earnings record, and the payroll recap sheet. By using the Todd System, or a similar device, this is done in one step. After all three forms are placed on the device, the payroll clerk fills in the check stub from gross pay to net pay, and the information is transposed on the earnings record and the recap sheet by the system. The clerk foots and cross foots the payroll recap sheet. The checks are run through the protector and on payday they are received by the employees. Payroll totals, by departments, are posted to the ledger.

The various federal and state taxes cause additional headaches for the accounting department. Income tax and social security require quarterly filing of reports on money withheld from employees, and the amounts are paid monthly; in the case of social security, the employer's tax must also be reported and paid. Workmen's compensation is very similar to an insurance policy—the actual premium is based on the hotel's accident record for a given period. At the beginning of the year the premium is estimated and paid quarterly, and at the close of the year the actual rate is computed and the final quarterly payment adjusted accordingly. Unemployment insurance requires a maximum payment of 3 percent of total payroll. Of this amount, .3 of 1 percent goes to the federal government, and the remainder goes

FIGURE 45. *Statement of profit and loss.*

STATEMENT OF PROFIT AND LOSS

	Schedule Number	Aug.19-2	Aug.19-1	Three Months Ended Aug.31,19-2	Aug.31,19-1
ROOMS DEPARTMENT	(B-1)				
Revenue		$ 95,153.90	$ 89,732.50	$ 270,059.75	$ 259,628.00
Expenses		25,799.18	25,533.55	74,027.92	73,313.00
Rooms Department Profit		$ 69,354.72	$ 64,198.95	$ 196,031.83	$ 186,315.00
OTHER OPERATED DEPARTMENTS PROFIT OR (LOSS)					
Food and Beverage	(B-2)	$ 23,951.41	$ 23,224.62	$ 67,536.04	$ 69,247.82
Telephone	(B-3)	1,426.54	1,330.85	3,021.73	1,918.29
Barber Shop	(B-4)	731.81	547.46	1,941.05	1,566.18
Drug Store	(B-5)	188.09	585.44	1,028.96	1,474.95
Valet	(B-6)	347.37	258.86	2,213.49	2,124.67
Swimming Pool	(B-7)	(952.77)	(756.23)	(1,922.91)	(1,352.72)
Total Other Operated Departments Profits		$ 25,692.45	$ 25,191.00	$ 73,818.36	$ 74,979.19
TOTAL OPERATED DEPARTMENTS PROFITS		$ 95,047.17	$ 89,389.95	$ 269,850.19	$ 261,294.19
OTHER INCOME	(B-8)	1,495.26	1,887.80	6,691.38	6,704.25
GROSS OPERATING INCOME		$ 96,542.43	$ 91,277.75	$ 276,541.57	$ 267,998.44
GENERAL AND UNAPPORTIONED EXPENSES					
Administrative and General	(B-9)	$ 11,198.45	$ 11,548.66	$ 28,796.04	$ 28,280.13
Pay Roll Taxes and Employee Relations	(B-9)	5,378.21	4,850.01	15,892.50	14,430.30
Advertising and Business Promotion	(B-10)	4,552.60	3,509.88	17,431.62	12,682.61
Heat, Light and Power	(B-10)	7,010.50	6,027.91	20,389.85	18,061.15
Repairs and Maintenance	(B-11)	12,434.84	10,125.60	35,491.38	34,643.14
		$ 40,574.60	$ 36,062.06	$ 118,001.39	$ 108,097.33
HOUSE PROFIT		$ 55,967.83	$ 55,215.69	$ 158,540.18	$ 159,901.11
STORE RENTALS		4,050.00	4,050.00	12,150.00	12,150.00
NET OPERATING INCOME		$ 60,017.83	$ 59,265.69	$ 170,690.18	$ 172,051.11
INSURANCE AND TAXES					
Fire Insurance		$ 228.19	$ 228.19	$ 684.53	$ 684.57
Real Estate and Personal Property Taxes - Estimated		5,669.37	5,887.10	17,008.11	17,715.30
		$ 5,897.56	$ 6,115.29	$ 17,692.64	$ 18,399.87
PROFIT AVAILABLE FOR INTEREST AND DEPRECIATION		$ 54,120.27	$ 53,150.40	$ 152,997.54	$ 153,651.24
INTEREST					
Interest on Mortgage Indebtedness		1,500.00	1,650.00	4,500.00	4,950.00
PROFIT AVAILABLE FOR DEPRECIATION		$ 52,620.27	$ 51,500.40	$ 148,497.54	$ 148,701.24
DEPRECIATION		12,027.96	12,479.37	35,000.80	37,328.30
PROFIT BEFORE INCOME TAXES		$ 40,592.31	$ 39,021.03	$ 113,496.74	$ 111,372.94
INCOME TAXES - Estimated		21,000.00	20,000.00	57,000.00	56,000.00
NET PROFIT FOR THE PERIOD		$ 19,592.31	$ 19,021.03	$ 56,496.74	$ 55,372.94

to the state. Most states now have a form of merit rating which determines how much of the 2.7 percent must be paid by the employer. The lower the turnover rate, the lower the unemployment insurance tax for the individual employer. The only remaining duty of the payroll clerk comes at the close of the year. The individual employee W-4 Withholding Statement must be filled out and sent to the employee. Information for this form is transcribed from the individual earnings records.

The busiest period of the accounting office begins on the first of each month, since the books are closed at the end of the month and then the financial statements must be prepared. (Any attempt

FIGURE 46. *Comparative balance sheet.*

COMPARATIVE BALANCE SHEET
as of Aug. 31, 19-2 and Aug. 31, 19-1

ASSETS	Aug.31,19-2	Aug.31,19-1	Increase (Decrease)
CURRENT ASSETS			
Cash			
House Funds	$ 7,500.00	$ 7,500.00	$ -
Bank - Regular Account	326,499.99	309,953.68	16,546.31
Bank - Exchange Account	1,500.00	1,500.00	-
Bank - Pay Roll Account	3,000.00	2,500.00	500.00
	$338,499.99	$321,453.68	$17,046.31
Accounts Receivable			
Guest Ledger	$ 18,326.44	$ 16,560.19	$ 1,766.25
City Ledger	69,136.34	72,265.51	(3,129.17)
	$ 87,462.78	$ 88,825.70	$(1,362.92)
less: Reserve for Bad Debts	8,035.60	8,044.59	(8.99)
	$ 79,427.18	$ 80,781.11	$(1,353.93)
Inventories			
Food	$ 5,417.49	$ 5,336.17	$ 81.32
Liquor and Beverage	15,889.82	18,223.64	(2,333.82)
Supplies	4,625.02	4,049.03	575.99
	$ 25,932.33	$ 27,608.84	$(1,676.51)
Prepaid Expenses			
Insurance and Licenses	7,295.75	8,408.05	$ (1,112.30)
Other Expenses	1,922.01	1,603.22	318.79
	$ 9,217.76	$ 10,011.27	$ (793.51)
Total Current Assets	$ 453,077.26	$ 439,854.90	$ 13,222.36
INVESTMENTS			
Investment in B-Hotel Co.	$ 300,000.00	$ 300,000.00	$ -
FIXED ASSETS			
Land	$ 300,000.00	$ 300,000.00	$ -
Buildings	$1500,000.00	$1500,000.00	$ -
less: Reserve for Depreciation	750,000.00	700,000.00	50,000.00
	$ 750,000.00	$ 800,000.00	$(50,000.00)
Furniture, Fixtures, Carpets and Drapes	$ 909,510.50	$ 870,796.65	$ 38,713.85
less: Reserve for Depreciation	657,671.33	590,276.28	67,395.05
	$ 251,839.17	$ 280,520.37	$(28,681.20)
Machinery and Equipment	$ 634,222.22	$ 605,777.77	28,444.45
less: Reserve for Depreciation	442,111.11	416,777.77	25,333.34
	$ 192,111.11	$ 189,000.00	$ 3,111.11
Operating Equipment - (Net of Reserves)	$ 131,725.30	$ 132,844.43	$ (1,119.13)
Total Fixed Assets	$1625,675.58	$1702,364.80	$(76,689.22)
DEFERRED EXPENSES			
Advertising Expense	$ 12,765.00	$ 8,425.00	$ 4,340.00
TOTAL ASSETS	$2391,517.84	$2450,644.70	$(59,126.86)

LIABILITIES	Aug.31,19-2	Aug.31,19-1	Increase (Decrease)
CURRENT LIABILITIES			
Accounts Payable	$ 121,944.94	$ 110,342.38	$ 11,602.56
Notes payable	-	50,000.00	(50,000.00)
	$ 121,944.94	$ 160,342.38	$(38,397.44)
Accrued Expenses			
Salaries and Wages	$ 36,100.73	$ 35,697.15	$ 403.58
Withholding and Pay Roll Taxes	12,553.04	12,515.50	37.54
Cabaret and Sales Taxes	2,922.30	2,871.00	51.30
Telephone Expense	5,554.80	5,201.72	353.08
Utilities	1,456.53	1,484.47	(27.94)
Interest on Mortgage Indebtedness	4,500.00	4,950.00	(450.00)
Other Expenses	814.63	1,800.40	(985.77)
	$ 63,902.03	$ 64,520.24	$ (618.21)
Accrued Taxes -			
Estimated Income Taxes	$ 57,000.00	$ 56,000.00	$ 1,000.00
Real Estate and Personal Property Taxes	45,354.96	47,096.80	(1,741.84)
	$ 102,354.96	$ 103,096.80	$ (741.84)
Mortgage Payment due within one year	$ 40,000.00	$ 40,000.00	$ -
Total Current Liabilities	$ 328,201.93	$ 367,959.42	$(39,757.49)
MORTGAGE INDEBTEDNESS			
First Mortgage - payable in yearly installments of $40,000.00 plus accrued interest on May 31 of each year less: Next Payment shown as current liability	$ 400,000.00	$ 440,000.00	$(40,000.00)
	40,000.00	40,000.00	-
	$ 360,000.00	$ 400,000.00	$(40,000.00)
STOCKHOLDERS' EQUITY			
12,000 shares of common capital stock at $100.00 par value	$1200,000.00	$1200,000.00	$ -
Retained Earnings at May 31, 19-2	446,819.17	427,312.34	19,506.83
Profit for the Fiscal Year to Date	56,496.74	55,372.94	1,123.80
	$1703,315.91	$1682,685.28	$ 20,630.63
TOTAL LIABILITIES AND CAPITAL	$2391,517.84	$2450,644.70	$(59,126.86)

to explain the procedures of closing the books and preparing the statements is beyond the scope of this treatment.) The three principal statements are the statement of earned surplus, the statement of profit and loss, and the balance sheet. The reader may gain a picture of two of these statements by observing Figures 45 and 46. Although our example hotel is a representative 300-room hotel, there is no such thing as an average or typical 300-room hotel.

Statistical Reports

Once the financial statements are out of the way, the office turns its attention to the compilation of the statistical reports that are necessary to successful hotel operation. The number and type of reports will vary from hotel to hotel, but most common are period comparisons on rooms, food, and beverage, both in dollars and in percentages. The usual comparison is the current month with the same month last year, or this year to date with last year to date or this three-months' period with the same period last year. Figure 47 illustrates the dollar report for the rooms department, and Figue 48 shows the identical information on a percentage basis. Similar reports are compiled for the food and beverage departments. A second group of reports is concerned with room statistics, food statistics, and payroll statistics. The room statistics report is shown in Figure 49.

Sound business practice dictates that every firm have its books audited by an outside firm every six months or at least once each year. Because, in certain phases, hotel accounting differs from general accounting, two accounting firms in the United States—Harris, Kerr Forster Company, and Horwath and Horwath—specialize in hotel accounting services. Both firms employ auditors who travel to the hotels and perform the audit. If a hotel prefers to have a man assigned full time, the firm charges a set fee and handles the typing and compilation of all statements and statistics in its central office, thus saving the hotel

ROOMS DEPARTMENT			Three Months Ended	
	Aug.19-2	Aug.19-1	Aug.31,19-2	Aug.31,19-1
REVENUE				
Transient	$ 92,375.70	$ 86,832.50	$ 261,861.55	$ 250,928.00
Permanent	2,778.20	2,900.00	8,198.20	8,700.00
Total Revenue	$ 95,153.90	$ 89,732.50	$ 270,059.75	$ 259,628.00
EXPENSES				
Salaries and Wages				
Front Office	$ 3,538.89	$ 3,419.70	$ 10,454.81	$ 9,915.57
Housekeeping	12,119.70	11,578.44	34,296.06	33,637.62
Service	2,916.78	2,859.75	8,755.95	8,493.71
	$ 18,575.37	$ 17,857.89	$ 53,506.82	$ 52,046.90
Employees' Meals	546.11	605.95	1,613.19	1,495.97
Uniforms	251.12	333.67	856.46	1,063.45
Laundry	2,435.50	2,726.70	7,074.31	7,028.28
Linen Replacements	951.54	897.33	2,700.60	2,596.32
Kitchenette Equipment	-	-	46.55	-
Cleaning Supplies	927.01	575.73	1,535.51	2,049.67
Dry Cleaning	284.75	298.77	925.15	781.42
Guest Supplies	1,069.56	1,321.68	2,715.76	4,315.48
Printing and Stationery	353.65	316.63	1,943.34	657.35
Telephone and Telegraph	122.25	104.41	301.37	301.34
Flowers and Decorations	23.60	252.53	173.66	395.90
Travel Agents' Commissions	117.80	40.80	245.62	111.95
Equipment Rental	108.88	198.45	341.88	465.96
Miscellaneous	32.04	3.01	47.70	3.01
Total Expenses	$ 25,799.18	$ 25,533.55	$ 74,027.92	$ 73,313.00
DEPARTMENTAL PROFIT	$ 69,354.72	$ 64,198.95	$ 196,031.83	$ 186,315.00

FIGURE 47. *Dollar report for the rooms department.*

ROOMS DEPARTMENT - PERCENTAGES			Three Months Ended	
	Aug.19-2	Aug. 19-1	Aug.31,19-2	Aug.31,19-1
REVENUE				
Transient	97.1 %	96.8 %	97.0 %	96.6 %
Permanent	2.9	3.2	3.0	3.4
Total Revenue	100.0 %	100.0 %	100.0 %	100.0 %
EXPENSES				
Salaries and Wages				
Front Office	3.7 %	3.8 %	3.9 %	3.8 %
Housekeeping	12.7	12.9	12.7	12.9
Service	3.1	3.2	3.2	3.3
	19.5 %	19.9 %	19.8 %	20.0 %
Employees' Meals	.6	.7	.6	.6
Uniforms	.3	.4	.3	.4
Laundry	2.6	3.0	2.6	2.7
Linen Replacements	1.0	1.0	1.0	1.0
Kitchenette Equipment	-	-	-	-
Cleaning Supplies	1.0	.6	.6	.8
Dry Cleaning	.3	.3	.3	.3
Guest Supplies	1.0	1.5	1.0	1.7
Printing and Stationery	.5	.4	.7	.3
Telephone and Telegraph	.1	.1	.1	.1
Flowers and Decorations	-	.3	.1	.1
Travel Agents' Commissions	.1	.1	.1	-
Equipment Rental	.1	.2	.1	.2
Miscellaneous	-	-	.1	-
Total Expenses	27.1 %	28.5 %	27.4 %	28.2 %
DEPARTMENTAL PROFIT	72.9 %	71.5 %	72.6 %	71.8 %

FIGURE 48. *Percentage report for the rooms department.*

ROOMS STATISTICS

	Aug.19-2	Aug.19-1	Three Months Ended Aug.31,19-2	Aug.31,19-1
TOTAL AVAILABLE ROOMS PER DAY	285	285	285	285
TOTAL AVAILABLE ROOMS FOR THE PERIOD	8,835	8,835	25,650	25,650
ROOMS OCCUPIED AND VACANT				
Occupied by Guests				
Transient	8,277	8,049	23,085	22,944
Permanent	312	341	899	990
Total Rooms Occupied by Guests	8,589	8,390	23,984	23,934
Complimentary	20	21	40	114
House Use	226	335	651	895
Vacant	-	89	975	707
	8,835	8,835	25,650	25,650
PERCENTAGE OF ROOMS OCCUPIED AND VACANT				
Occupied by Guests				
Transient	93.7 %	91.1 %	90.0 %	89.4 %
Permanent	3.5	3.9	3.5	3.9
Total Rooms Occupied by Guests	97.2 %	95.0 %	93.5 %	93.3 %
Complimentary	.2	.2	.2	.5
House Use	2.6	3.8	2.5	3.5
Vacant	-	1.0	3.8	2.7
	100.0 %	100.0 %	100.0 %	100.0 %
REVENUE				
Transient	$ 92,375.70	$ 86,832.50	$ 261,861.55	$ 250,928.00
Permanent	2,778.20	2,900.00	8,198.20	8,700.00
Total Revenue	$ 95,153.90	$ 89,732.50	$ 270,059.75	$ 259,628.00
AVERAGE REVENUE PER OCCUPIED ROOM PER DAY				
Transient	$ 11.16	$ 10.79	$ 11.34	$ 10.94
Permanent	8.90	8.50	9.12	8.79
Total Average	11.08	10.70	11.26	10.85
NUMBER OF GUESTS				
Transient	10,280	10,297	29,472	30,212
Permanent	341	372	959	1,080
Total Guests	10,621	10,669	30,431	31,292
AVERAGE REVENUE PER GUEST PER DAY				
Transient	$ 8.99	$ 8.43	$ 8.89	$ 8.30
Permanent	8.15	7.80	8.55	8.05
Total Average	8.96	8.41	8.87	8.30

FIGURE 49. *Rooms statistics report.*

many dollars. The resident auditor is paid by his firm, not by the hotel. In large hotels that employ food and beverage controllers, many of these men are placed in the hotel by the accounting firms and operate on the same basis as the resident auditors. Both Harris, Kerr Forster Company and Horwath and Horwath do special studies for hotels on food cost, scheduling, payroll control, and in hundreds of other areas. Each firm also publishes yearly statistics on the hotel industry and forecasts trends that are developing in the business.

While I have made no attempt here to explore the techniques and procedural methods of accounting as such, it is hoped that you have gained a picture of the work involved and an appreciation of the importance of the accounting function to successful hotel management.

CHAPTER 6

The Sales Department

Hotel sales management is a relative newcomer to the field of hotel management. New as it is, sales has become one of the most vital functions of hotelkeeping and is now considered an integral part of management. Not every hotel has a sales department or a sales manager, but the sales function is being performed in the greatest majority of them.

A recent statement by Ernest Henderson III, President of the Sheraton Corporation, will further emphasize the vital role of sales in today's hotel economy. He stated, "In England, if a man wants to reach the presidency of an organization, he usually goes through the financial division. In Germany, the fastest road up is through production. In the United States, the glory road is through sales and marketing."

In the Hilton Corporation, every new management trainee will have his first assignment as a sales representative. Obviously, Hilton believes in sales-minded managers.

DEVELOPMENT

The rapid growth and development of hotel sales management has resulted from a variety of influences and changes both in the industry and in the national economy. During and immediately following World War II, business was excellent and hotelmen enjoyed a seller's market. By 1948, however, occupancy figures began to decline, and hotels had vacant rooms far too often to yield a favorable profit picture. From a high average of 92 percent occupancy in 1946 the figures dropped to an average of 63 percent occupancy in the mid 1960's. Obviously, something had to be done to halt this trend and win back some of the lost business. It is true that the decline in occupancy has been partially offset by increased rates, but it is also generally agreed that room rates have now approached the maximum the public will pay and that any further increase might merely accelerate the downward trend. The situation calls for increasing rooms business, which is essentially a selling job.

The hotel industry traditionally has suffered from periods of dull business activity. In commercial hotels, weekends show very low rates of occupancy, and it is not unusual to have half of the rooms vacant on Saturday and Sunday nights. The general feeling among hotel managers has been that poor weekend business is unavoidable and an occupational hazard. Only recently, prodded by increasing costs and lower operating profits, has management concentrated on *promoting* weekend business.

In addition to weekend lulls, most hotels have a season of the year during which business is relatively weak. In the East, Midwest, and South, summer is a period of light business; during the months of June, July, and August, hotels in these areas are fortunate to break even. This point is well illustrated by a large New York hotel I recently visited during the summer—this 1,800-room hotel reported 1,000 vacant rooms for a Sunday night in July.

Increased competition has provided the greatest impetus to the development of hotel sales management. It is no secret that motels have sliced away a good portion of hotel rooms business, and if we add to this the increased competition between hotels themselves, it becomes evident that counteractive measures must be taken immediately if the hotels are to stay in the black. To win back the trade lost to motels or to replace it with new customers is a selling job.

Another reason for the development of sales management in the hotel industry can be found in the changing role played by the hotel manager. In former days the hotel manager played the role of "Mine Host," the genial greeter, the handshaker, the public relations type of individual. As the industry has developed and as economic influences have changed, the manager has, of necessity, relinquished his front position and has become a business executive whose primary concerns are statistics and percentages on rooms, food, payroll, and general administration. As a result of this change, public relations duties have been shouldered by the sales department. Today the sales manager and his staff are the principal guest contact men of the hotel industry.

The realization that food service is more than a necessary side line on which a hotel is fortunate to break even has also stimulated the growth of the sales department. The industry now recognizes that good food can increase rooms business and, at the same time, be a revenue producer.

The final reason for increased emphasis on sales is that in business today no firm can take its present trade for granted. Hotel managers realize that their competitors are continually wooing their patrons with ardent fervor and that no matter how favorable present business is or future trends appear to be, unless they apply some sales effort business will fall off. The American public is advertising conscious, and it is absolutely necessary to keep a firm in the public eye if it is to continue as a successful operation.

ORGANIZATION

The organization of a hotel sales department depends upon a variety of factors such as size and location of the hotel, the abilities and responsibilities of the staff, and the policy of the manager. In small hotels the manager is the sales manager. He supervises the sales work and, in most cases, passes on the actual jobs to be done by other people in the organization. This is the ideal situation because planning and administration of the sales program by one person should guarantee a coordinated, cohesive sales effort. In a large hotel the manager can no longer direct the sales program, the sales effort becomes scattered among several departments, and the danger of an uncoordinated program increases. If an uncoordinated program becomes a reality it creates poor liaison between the convention manager and banquet manager or between newspaper advertising and direct mail. To prevent such difficulties, leading sales experts recommend an organization in which all of the following departments are under the direct responsibility of the director of sales:

Front Office	Guest History Department
Banquet Department	Advertising Office
Convention Department	Publicity Office
General Food and Beverage Promotion	All Internal Selling

One person—the sales manager, or whoever else is designated by management—should have absolute authority over these departments to produce the tightly knit program that is essential. Many times two groups may want the same date for a convention, and it should then be the responsibility of the head of the sales department to evaluate the booking and decide which group is the more valuable. If he is unable to do so, the decision should be up to the general manager.

C. DeWitt Coffman, a leading hotel sales expert, lists the following specific responsibilities for any hotel sales department:

Sales planning
Sales policies
Sales budget
Interdepartmental
    cooperation
Research
Training
Selling stimulus

Sales department
    management
Personal selling
Display advertising
Publicity
Internal selling
Direct mail
General advertising

In fulfilling these responsibilities, the sales department operates in the three divisions of customer relations, trade relations, and staff relations. Customer relations is the biggest division, but if the work in this area is to be successful the hotel must maintain good will and contact with other members of the business, and interdepartmental cooperation within the hotel is mandatory. The sales department brings the business to the house, but the staff must produce the service and earn the satisfaction and good will of the customers.

ROOMS BUSINESS

A hotel has three products to sell: rooms, food, and beverages. Of these three, the most profitable is rooms. You have learned that room occupancy has taken a downward trend and that most hotels have slack periods of business both weekly and yearly.

How, then, does the sales department go about combating these difficulties?

Conventions

One of the best answers to slack rooms is the convention. A hotel sales department is continually alert to the possibility of booking a convention into the hotel, and in this area cooperation among the hotels of a city and also with the local chamber of commerce is imperative. As I have mentioned earlier, cities realize the value of convention business, and many of them have formed bureaus to actively promote this business. In such a venture, a city depends upon its hotels to guarantee suitable rooms and food. Conversely, the hotels depend upon the city, since large auditoriums so necessary to convention activities are usually under municipal jurisdiction. The hotels and the city convention bureau must therefore work very closely and pool their efforts in order to develop a program that will be attractive enough to sell the officers of a convention group on their city. Convention booking and selling is a highly competitive field because cities all over the country strive to attract business to their particular locale.

Few people realize the magnitude of the number of conventions that take place in this country every year. Local, state, national, and international conventions are continually being held. Yearly meetings are held by national associations, union groups, fraternities and sororities, educational associations, professional groups, veterans' groups, fraternal orders, national advertisers, and corporations of all types. And these represent only a sample of the prospective customers available to the hotel sales manager. Perhaps a few figures will give you a better idea of the potential in conventions.

Each year over 20,000 conventions are held in the United States. Over 10 million people are in attendance at these conventions. Last year New York City alone attracted over 900 conventions, attended by more than 2,000,000 delegates. In 1956 New

York opened its new 35 million dollar Coliseum to service conventions better. Within ten years there were complaints that it was too small and inadequate to handle New York's convention potential.

In recent years two giant (2,000 rooms each) hotels—The Americana and the The New York Hilton—have been built almost side by side in New York City. A quick glance at the layout and facilities of these hotels will demonstrate that conventions are the number one market for both of them.

Convention business has proven beneficial to hotels other than the commercial hotel. Resort hotels are entering the picture in greater numbers every year. Resorts have always been plagued by their relatively short season of operation wherein a bad break in the weather can easily turn profit into loss. Add to these handicaps the rising costs of operation, the increasing trend to travel vacations, and European competition, which is made even stronger by lower air travel rates, and the result is a business facing the very real prospect of bankruptcy. To counteract these evils, resorts are extending their open season at both ends by booking conventions before and after the regular season. This arrangement has been a great help to them, and convention delegates find resorts very pleasant sites for their operations.

Although convention business has boosted rooms revenue and bolstered sagging occupancy figures, it is not without its headaches for the hotel operator. Ideally, for the hotel, a convention should come during a slack period in business, but of course not all business executives desire to hold their conventions at times that are the most suitable for hotels. The sales manager must attempt to sell dates that are the most beneficial to his hotel, but in certain cases he will be forced to choose between losing a convention or booking it for a period when the hotel will be relatively busy with regular business. This is not an easy choice to make. A convention means good revenue, but if booking it means turning down regular customers the possible loss of their future business must be considered. Also to be considered are patrons of the hotel who aren't convention delegates. Most guests are not too happy when they learn there is to be a convention in the hotel, since to them it means the possibility of noise and revelry during early morning hours. In this respect, probably the least happy person to learn of a convention in his hotel is the resort guest. Resort operators do their best to keep convention business out of their regular season but some overlap is unavoidable. As one resort operator put it, "Our regular guests resent the conventions and look upon the delegates as intruders, but they should realize that without the conventions there probably would be no resort to come back to every year."

Conventions can add to the costs of operation. As a general rule, convention delegates cause more breakage and more room damage than the regular guest, though this destructive trend is on the downgrade because of stricter control imposed on the delegates by their national organizations. Another possible danger is that the sales manager or his representative may not know when to say "no" in pursuing a convention booking. To book a group that will not allow the hotel a profit is seldom considered good business.

Customer Relations

While conventions represent an important segment of the rooms business, the greatest bulk of room revenue still comes from individual customers. The sales manager and his staff continuously strive to gain repeat business from old customers and to find new guests for the hotel, and a hotel sales department leaves no stone unturned in its effort to make every visitor to the city conscious of its hotel and the fine accommodations and service it offers. This is a big job and one that can never be completely accomplished, but the sales personnel always strive for this unattainable goal.

Repeat business is good business and indicates to management that their past service has been satisfactory. An especially wise move is to make regular customers of people who are frequent visitors to the city. The best way to achieve this is for the staff to render such fine service that a guest would never think of staying anywhere else. The good salesman never takes this satisfaction for granted, however, and he always maintains contact with the guest, taking special care to handle complaints immediately. Many hotels even solicit comments from guests through forms placed in the rooms. The correct and prompt handling of complaints is vital because it seems human for a dissatisfied person to make his feelings known to everyone with whom he comes into contact. One complaint can do more harm than ten compliments can do good, and the old adage about one rotten apple spoiling the whole barrel is especially true. No good hotelman desires a situation that will cause dissatisfaction, but he has learned that skillful handling of complaints can often be a very effective selling tool. All sales departments must be complaint conscious.

Advertising

Obviously the sales department cannot personally call on everyone who has been a guest in the hotel; nevertheless, some degree of contact should be maintained. Most hotels keep a guest history file which serves as the information center for any direct mail advertising the hotel may do. It is most important that this guest history file be kept up to date. Direct mail advertising, when skillfully carried out, is an excellent means of promoting repeat business. Some hotels have a form that guests may fill out so that an announcement of his visit will appear in his hometown newspaper. Because most people love to see their names in print, they will remember the hotel favorably, and since the name of the hotel appears in the news item, this bit of free advertising may attract other customers from the same community.

In seeking new customers for the hotel, the sales department employs many tools, procedures, and techniques. If sales effort is to be expended, in what area or areas should it be directed to obtain maximum results? Where are the potential customers of a particular hotel? To answer these questions the sales manager utilizes market surveys, the guest history file, and any other leads he can find. With the market area outlined, the department then goes into action.

To reach the individual customer, advertisements may be placed in newspapers or magazines that appear in the particular market area. In designing and placing such advertisements the hotel usually employs a professional agency, which may work on a yearly fee basis or charge for the individual projects it handles for the hotel. Another type of advertising widely used by hotels is the roadside billboard. Strategically placed on principal highways leading into a city, these outdoor billboards can be very instrumental in producing room, food, and function business. With hotels now battling the motels for family business, such signs become increasingly important because the hotels' program is presented to the family as they approach the city. On these billboards many hotels stress, both in illustration and text, that the hotel is the perfect place for the entire family.

With the advent of television, hotel salespeople have at their disposal another means for attracting guests. Although buying time on a nationwide network is too expensive, and although advertising through local stations is more practicable but fails to reach a wide enough audience to be of much benefit to rooms business, local television advertising is used to promote other hotel services. Sales departments also constantly seek ways to get their hotel's name on network television without paying the high advertising rates, and here the much maligned quiz or giveaway program has proven to be of some value. One hotel gave a week or a weekend holiday for two as one of the prizes on a local program, and thus the hotel and its location were prominently mentioned on the show. Most hotel salespeople agree that this type of advertising is both effective and very reasonable in cost. Radio advertising is also used by hotels, but usually only for spot announcements. As in the case of television, this too is an expensive medium. In the same vein as free television advertising are newspaper and magazine articles that mention or feature the hotel. The sales manager must always be alert to situations which are news and which can benefit the hotel through publication.

Other Business Sources

Advertising is very necessary but by itself it does not fulfill the needs of hotel sales. The sales force must continuously sell *in person*, and must seek other contacts that will provide business for the hotel. Contacts with all transportation companies that service the city are especially important. Because agents of the airlines, railroads, and bus companies are always asked for information pertaining to hotels, the sales department must work through these representatives in order to gain business from the traveling public. A hotel may often arrange a package plan with a transportation company, in which the company sells the customer a package that included transportation, lodgings, and often certain recreational attractions. In small cities, a hotel frequently seeks the assistance of automobile service station owners. Motorists invariably stop at service stations for information, and if the operator can recommend a particular hotel many people will accept his recommendation. Some hotels pay a commission for this "recommended business" while others do not. Another excellent source of business is the travel agent. Each person or group booked through a travel agent costs the hotel a commission, but travel agents handle a large volume of travelers and most hotels find it good business to work closely with them. Closely related to travel agents are the many companies that sponsor tours of all types, the majority of which take place during the summer months when business is slow. A tour company expects low rates, but in return it can guarantee a hotel a certain volume of business and usually one or two meals for the tour group.

Most sales departments now emphasize "guaranteed reservations." This means the hotel sales representative contacts large companies that periodically send salesmen, engineers, or representatives to a city on business and offers the company a program that guarantees a room in the hotel (and usually guarantees a certain rate). If enough companies are signed up, a good flow of rooms business is assured. During busy seasons this program can cause difficulties and reduce, to some extent, the room revenue per guest, but the steady business during slack periods more than compensates for this.

PUBLIC SPACE

While room sales are the most profitable, the sales manager and his staff cannot devote all of their time to them. Hotels also have space for sale. Hotel statisticians have developed formulas that tell how much revenue each square foot of a hotel should yield, and pressure is always on the sales department to produce these amounts. All hotels have public space, although the exact amount and distribution varies tremendously from one hotel to another even of the same size. Public space consists of private dining rooms, banquet rooms, ballrooms, meeting rooms, or any other region of the hotel that can be financially productive. Most of the potential business for such space is local, and sales representatives, in trying to sell this space, must call on businessmen for business and sales meetings; solicit officers of all types of organizations for banquets; and strive to sell individuals on the advantages of holding specific functions in the hotel. Dances should be eagerly sought, and many hotels specialize in wedding receptions. The hotel sales representative should also actively solicit other functions such as company award dinners, office parties, and holiday celebrations.

The size and nature of a hotel's public space are the controlling factors in function promotion by the sales department. Too little space, the absence of large banquet rooms, and lack of a meeting room with large seating capactiy can, of course, be tremendous handicaps. Seldom can a hotel undergo the physical changes necessary to alter these handicaps, so too often the sales department must watch profitable functions go to a competitor simply because he has the room to accommodate a group. It is possible for a hotel to have so much public space that it cannot be consistently filled, but the great majority of hotels have too little rather than too much. While conventions usually help all hotels in a city, the hotel with the best public space accommodations is the one that becomes convention headquarters and the one that profits most.

Good convention and function accommodations can provide a real lift to rooms business too. One of the best illustrations of this point is the Sheraton Park, in Washington, D.C. When Sheraton purchased this hotel the building had a large number of guest rooms but very little function and meeting space. Room revenue was poor, and business was going downhill. The chain built a million dollar ballroom addition to the hotel, which has done an excellent function business and given a definite upswing to the rooms revenue. Thus, the Sheraton Park has changed from a disintegrating property to a thriving, healthy hotel.

Another innovation in function business recently introduced by the Sheraton Corporation was the installation of closed circuit television in all hotels of the chain, thereby establishing a network that covers every major city in the United States. If a manufacturer wishes to have a national showing of his new line of merchandise it is no longer necessary to have all of the prospective customers gathered in one city. A meeting is held in each city, and those present view the product on a large television screen. This has proven valuable for sales meetings of companies whose people are distributed over a wide area, since rental of the Sheraton facilities is less expensive than the travel costs of bringing the people to one meeting point. Political groups can hold fund raising dinners throughout the country simultaneously, the principal speaker being present at each dinner via the closed circuit television network. From all indications, closed circuit television is an excellent revenue producer. Everyday Sheraton discovers new possibilities for this idea in hotelkeeping.

The old adage, "A salesman must know his product," is very appropriate for hotel sales personnel, especially in public space promotion. A salesman should possess a thorough knowledge of room layout and capacity, number, type, and rates of guest rooms, menu pricing, special abilities of the culinary department, and the various services the hotel can offer. Equally important is an ability and willingness to confer and cooperate with the various department heads involved in the preparation and provision of any function he may sell. As is true of most areas of hotelkeeping, success in the final analysis depends entirely upon cooperation among all departments of the organization. Because of this, it is generally believed that the *hotel* sales representative holds one of the most difficult and challenging positions in the entire field of selling.

SERVICES PROMOTION

The duties of the sales department do not end with the selling of rooms and public space. Every hotel has guest services that must be promoted, and this internal selling is highly important. The principal services to be sold include entertainment, valet and room service, the restaurants, cocktail lounge, specialty rooms and shops in the hotel, and, in the case of chain operation, other hotels in the group. Hotel guests are a captive audience for this type of sales promotion.

The clustering of restaurants, diners, taverns, and, to a lesser extent, package stores in the immediate neighborhood of most hotels is not a coincidence. Owners of these businesses actively seek and enjoy the patronage of hotel guests. Many hotel guests commonly have the impression, rightly or wrongly, that hotel dining rooms are too expensive or too formal; as a result, during meal hours there is a small exodus from the hotels to nearby restaurants. To retain or regain this food business for the hotel is primarily a job of internal selling, and hotels have taken positive steps by offering food services in a variety of settings and at all price levels. The heretofore plush, formal dining room is nearly passé, and a volume food business is now done in the coffee shop, in the specialty rooms, in the "minute chef," or over the drugstore counter. Needless to say, the mere existence of these services and facilities is not enough—they must be promoted, and promotion is the responsibility of the sales department.

In reality, internal selling has the most ideal sales setup of any of the areas in which the sales department works. The person *in* the hotel is a prime sales prospect, and "All selling is really just a substitute for sampling" is certainly true, because when a guest is *in* the hotel he is already sampling some of the services. Other businesses continually use the "hooker" or loss leader to attract potential customers, knowing that once a person is there he can usually be sold other items as well. In internal selling not only is the guest present, but the best method of selling—personal contact—can be utilized. Perhaps the greatest asset of internal sales is that every dollar sale represents additional income at little or no added promotion cost.

Hotels have a variety of tools and techniques at their disposal for internal selling: criss-cross advertising, guest service directories in the rooms, tent cards on tables, lobby displays, elevator cards and bulletin boards. While all of these ideas are good and will sell a certain number of guests, there is no substitute for personal, face-to-face selling. In internal selling, every guest contact employee is a potential salesman and is in the most favorable position to perform the sales function. In one day such employees talk to a hundred times as many guests as the manager does in one month. Realizing this, many hotels give employees sales training and develop campaigns centered on employee selling. The goal is to make every employee a salesman.

Part Three

The Future: Opportunities and Trends

CHAPTER 7

Career Opportunities
in the Hotel Industry

Hotelkeeping is a broad and complex business that provides career opportunities for persons of almost every age, experience, and education. Like all businesss it has, as mentioned earlier, characteristic advantages and disadvantages that should be carefully considered by anyone contemplating a hotel career.

Without reiterating the disadvantages, its primary advantages are interesting work, good chances of advancement, generally excellent working surroundings, social contact, security, and stability of employment. In most hotel positions there is an absence of assembly line monotony and the presence of frequent opportunities to meet and serve all segments of the public. Hotel work provides ample opportunity for the employee to use his initiative and to express his ideas. For those with managerial, executive, and ownership aspirations, the hotel industry ranks high in opportunity among all the nation's businesses. Add to these advantages the important role played by hotels in the local, state, and national scene, and you have the basic reasons for considering a hotel career.

JOB LEVELS

In the short space of this chapter it would be impossible to list all the possible jobs in the hotel industry. Instead, representative jobs on three different levels of skill and training have been selected. The first level contains the unskilled and semiskilled jobs, which require no previous experience or specialized preparation. (These are entry jobs.) The second level contains the skilled jobs, which require experience and/or specialized training. The third or top level contains the supervisory, executive, and managerial positions, which require the greatest amount of experience, training, and education.

Individuals with high school education or less and who have had no hotel or related experience should concentrate on the entry level jobs as a starting point for a hotel career. Every department has one or more job classifications at this level. No one should feel that starting here precludes the possibility of ever advancing very far upward in the organization, since the majority of today's hotel managers and executives began at this level. The experience gained in such initial positions plus the knowledge assimilated from training programs and contact with other jobs are steppingstones to positions in the second, or skilled, level of hotel work. The ambitious employee can enroll in the American Hotel Institute and take specialized hotel correspondence courses. The American Hotel Institute is a nonprofit extension service organized by the American Hotel Association and administered by Michigan State University.

Representative entry jobs are listed below by areas.

Front of the House

Bellman
Elevator Operator
Apprentice Telephone
   Operator
Porter

Food and Beverage Service

Busboy
Barboy

Secretarial

Clerk
Typist

Accounting

Checker
File Clerk

Food Preparation

Vegetable Preparer
Kitchen Helper
Pantry Girl
Storeroom Helper
Warewasher

Engineering

Plumber's Helper
Electrician's Helper
Oiler's Helper

Laundry

Washer
Extractor
Presser

Applicants for the second level, the skilled category, come from a variety of sources. Many of the positions are filled by employees moving up from the various entry jobs. Other people gain a skilled trade in another industry and then seek similar employment in a hotel. Graduates of technical schools and junior colleges giving hotel training fill a portion of these jobs, and others come from business schools or specialized high school training courses.

Perhaps a few examples will clarify this particular level. A person with no experience but a desire to work in food preparation should consider any of the schools that train cooks, bakers, and other food service personnel because graduates of these schools are in demand by hotels and other food service industries. (A list of such schools is given in the appendix.) Men who have had military food training can find direct employment in many hotel kitchens. Numerous hotels operate apprentice training programs in food preparation, and acceptance into such a program is an excellent start toward the knowledge and experience necessary for a successful career in hotel food preparation. For those interested in employment as bookkeepers, accounting clerks, secretaries, or accountants, training at a good business school is recommended. The jobs in the dining and banquet departments rely almost entirely on experience; the usual pathway is busboy—waiter—captain—headwaiter. The majority of bartenders are former waiters, although training in mixology can be obtained at some special schools. Room clerks and reservation clerks come from the ranks of the bellmen and from the technical schools. Training for the mechanical jobs in the housekeeping and engineering departments can be found outside as well as within the hotel industry. Plumbers, electricians, carpenters, painters, and upholsterers are usually union positions and have established apprenticeship programs. Anyone seeking employment in these areas should consult either the local unions or contractors employing these trades. Most applicants for such hotel positions attain a journeyman status in the trade before seeking hotel work.

The following list contains a representative sample of job classifications at the skilled level:

Secretary	Accountant	Waiter
Accounting	Room Clerk	Hostess
Clerk	Reservation	Headwaiter
Bookkeeper	Clerk	Night Auditor
Assistant House-	Floor House-	Fry Cook
keeper	keeper	Vegetable Cook
Plumber	Baker	Bartender

Electrician	Roast Cook	Receiving Clerk
Oiler	Garde de	Painter
Kitchen Steward	Manager	Telephone Oper-
Sales Represen-	Wine Steward	ator
tative	Carpenter	
Upholsterer	Waiter Captain	

Note that the skilled level encompasses several areas of responsibility, prestige, and salary. The above listed jobs vary accordingly and are not given in any particular order.

Training, experience, and individual initiative are the keys to the executive, managerial level. The current trend is to fill these postions with college trained men, but the door will never be slammed in the faces of qualified men who have worked their way up through the organization. Many department head jobs will always be filled primarily from the ranks of the skilled level.

Young people contemplating a hotel management career should, however, give serious consideration to college training. Many well-known colleges and universities now offer a complete four-year course in hotel management. (Names and addresses of such schools are listed in the appendix.) While this type of specialized college training is recommended, it is not absolutely mandatory; graduates of liberal arts schools and other colleges find hotel employment every year.

Even though a hotel school graduate assimilates a large amount of technical knowledge along with some practical experience during his four years of college, he is not ready for a manager's job upon graduation. Like the graduate of a medical school, he must serve an internship before engaging in actual practice. Both the length and nature of this internship are highly variable factors. Both depend upon the size and type of hotel, the training, experience, and interests of the graduate as well as his ability, and the availability of promotional opportunities.

What type of jobs do hotel school graduates obtain? The

large chain operations have graduate training programs for which they recruit college graduates. A trainee spends about one year in the program, during which time he gains experience in and knowledge of every department. Upon completion of the program he is assigned a regular job in the hotel and begins the climb to managerial and executive responsibilities. While this type of organized training program exists primarily in the metropolitan chain hotel, many hotel managers are anxious to obtain and develop young management material. The young graduate who does not enter a training program will usually start in one of the following, or similar, jobs: Steward, Assistant Manager, Sales Representative, Food and Beverage Controller, Receiving Clerk, Accountant, Assistant Food and Beverage Manager, Restaurant Manager.

Many college graduates, armed with four years of theoretical knowledge and technical know-how, become impatient when told they need experience before assuming high level positions of responsibility. What these young people fail to realize is that, though intellectually mature, they are not socially and emotionally developed to the degree necessary for managerial positions. The principal executive function of understanding, motivating, and directing people can be developed only through experience. It is vital that young men and women understand and accept this situation, or else their assets of enthusiasm, ambition, and confidence may disintegrate and be replaced by disillusionment, lethargy, and dissatisfaction.

Positions representative of the managerial or executive level of hotel management are:

Front Office	Credit Manager	Auditor
Manager	Executive Assist-	Chef
Controller	ant Manager	Chief Engineer
Executive	Convention	General
Housekeeper	Manager	Manager

Catering	Sales Manager	Banquet
Manager	Resident	Manager
Steward	Manager	
Food and Bever-	Personnel Direc-	
age Manager	tor	

SMALL HOTEL OR LARGE HOTEL

"Is it better to gain my experience in a small hotel or a large hotel?" is the question most often asked by hotel school students. While no pat answer can be given, the question deserves considerable attention. Two well-known and extremely successful hotelmen graciously consented to approach the question from opposite sides. Mr. Ruel Tyo, Executive Vice-President of Packard Hotels Company, presents the case for the small hotel. Mr. Wallace W. Lee, Executive Vice-President of the Howard Johnson Motor Lodges, analyzes the value of large hotel experience.

The Case for the Small Hotel

"Smaller hotels surpass the larger hotels for those aspiring to the role of entrepreneur. In the long run, the opportunty to be independent and to be a real boss is much more possible in the small hotel. Reading the trade publications will verify these statements. Since this may be contrary to what many young people think in this age of bigness, however, let us study the reasons behind my thinking.

"For many years after entering the profession of innkeeping, my ambition was to run a big hotel. After this dream became a reality, I realized that the returns were not in proportion to the efforts expended and the years of hard apprenticeship. For five years the thrill of running a 600-room hotel was mine; then I took stock and asked myself where I was going. Suppose one could save $3,000 net per year. Then in ten years, if all went well, the family bank book would show $30,000. That would be fine, but there were many 'ifs' to be considered. I had little, if any, security as manager, and changing big jobs is expensive. Assuming that the directors of our hotel would be satisfied with my stewardship, I still ran the risk of having the property sold out from under me. The new owners might have their own manager who would drop in one fine day to take over the reins. Big jobs don't hang on bushes, and presumably it would be necessary to pull up stakes and move to another big city, probably far away. That wouldn't cripple a career hotel man permanently, but how about my growing family? Leaving friends, changing schools and old familiar surroundings becomes more difficult after forty than at twenty or twenty-five.

"About this time, war broke out and the United States Navy took over our hotel. As fortune would have it, they left me in charge instead of taking over completely as they did in most instances. Right then and there I swapped horses and decided to look for a small hotel where I could have security and build up an equity for the future. That's another story, too long to tell here with all the details of making a lease, arranging for the financing, and so forth.

"Many young people worry needlessly about where to start on their hotel career. What branch of hotel operation is the best in which to start after graduation? Truly, it has been demonstrated many times that it doesn't matter too much how one starts, it's how one ends the game that counts.

"No two people are exactly alike. It is logical to assume, therefore, that they do not think alike. Later, in the business world, they will not operate alike. They will attempt to follow a pattern and work on a similar system, but it won't be exactly the same. *Initiative is what counts in the end result.* Don't fret about commencing in a different department or in a different type of hotel than the other fellow. Get on the job, give it the best you have, and later on, sit down, evaluate your present work, recapitulate your past experience, and then set a straight course for the goal you have decided upon.

"People we all know have risen to the top by starting in the back of the house, the front office, the sales department, the promotion department, or the service department. Just one look at the roster of the American Hotel Association past presidents will provide ample proof of this.

"One of the important things is to learn all phases of hotel operation and branch out later in the field that you like best. Get your apprentice work over with first *in those departments you know the least about*. The only sure-fire short-cut to the top is to marry the only daughter or son of a rich hotel owner!

"Seriously, the great American hotel business is the seventh largest industry in the United States. It is something to be proud of. Many people don't know that over 78 percent of this industry is made up of hotels with 125 rooms or less. The small hotel is the backbone of the hospitality business, the successor to the early inn. Many folks still think of small hotels as second rate establishments, but smaller hotels can be *good* hotels giving good, honest value and true hospitality. Younger men and women with formal training and farsightedness are greatly needed in this field. The job needs businessmen, not tavern keepers, as many were in the past. As smaller hotel businessmen, young people can become civic leaders in their respective localities, actively a somebody not just an anybody. The smaller hotel can be the focal point of community activity and the meeting place for both big and little people.

"Quoting from Jim Pearson, editor of the *Southern Hotel Journal*, 'When 81 percent of all hotels (in 1934) were in the hands of receivers, institutions, trustees, or banks, the 19 percent which were able to keep their financial heads above water were nearly all in the smaller hotel bracket. They averaged 75 rooms, so you can see that not many larger hotels could be included.'

"Only in the small hotel can one learn all phases of operation. Big houses have a tendency to develop specialists in one department or another. Still, a turn in the deluxe houses never hurt anyone. Young students or beginners can usually explore and investigate other departments more easily than an older person. But the old adage about all is not gold that glitters should be kept in mind. Those who are just starting out should not be blinded by the bright lights too long and perhaps lose sight of the solid things in life. Security, independence, comfortable home life, respect, dignity, and that sense of well-being that comes from a real job well done—all these can be found in running a smaller hotel in a smaller town.

"When young people prepare themselves properly for the role of entrepreneur, they should plan and expect to work out a round of apprenticeship after college. It is not reasonable or practical to be too hasty and expect to have everything at the beginning. Like doctors, good hotel students should expect to work out a modified internship, because at this stage learning the practical side of the business is paramount. Periodically, a check should be made by hotel folks on themselves against the good sound theories they learned from books. Then, if they feel they are on the right track, they can proceed full speed ahead.

"A good plan is to work for a recognized operator or a well known chain for a few years to polish off the rough edges of inexperience. Then, when the time comes to take the big jump independently, I would advise becoming an operator and not a trader of hotels. Actually, this usually gives the best returns in the long run, and there are not as many chances of getting out on a limb by over-expanding and underfinancing. As one moves into a city he should be sure to secure all the information possible as to the past and future of that city. After careful study and analysis of general business cycles, the investment can be made on the premise of a long stay. The community is very important. A famous host once said there were three important reasons behind the success of a business: (1) location, (2) location, and (3) location. The community must have a well balanced economy and an industry backed by a strong, prosperous agricultural region. A county seat and a college town enjoy weekend business. One should choose a city in which the citizens pull together, take good and bad times in their stride, and he will have a town that is going forward.

"In the final analysis, there are three ways to make good money: (1) with the hands plus hard work, (2) with the head plus special training. (3) with other people's capital. These three ways may best be combined in smaller hotel operation.

"For a final comment on smaller hotels, it might be well to remember that fifty years before the birth of Christ, Julius Caesar said it was better to be first in a little Iberian village than to be second in the great city of Rome."

The Case for the Large Hotel

While Mr. Tyo presented the case of the small hotel both as an initial training ground and as a career, Mr. Lee speaks primarily of the meaning and value of large hotel employment as a starting point for the embryo executive.

"It is true that any successful inn, small or large, becomes and remains successful through the coordination of individual efforts. However, the real difference between the two, small or large, seems to me to be the difference between a team in which the captain can personally lead each individual and one in which the captain must influence several levels and groups of supervisors—each of whom in turn carry out and extend the leadership —thus helping to produce the final results.

"Now let us consider the advantages of large hotel experience. The large hotel offers a more complete operation. The young trainee can gain experience in all phases of hotel operation and get a complete picture of the methods and intricacies involved in each function. Only from the large hotel can one gain well rounded experience.

"In the large hotel one has the opportunity to learn more quickly. Because of the multiplicity of functions, the young graduate can sample each and use this opportunity to find the areas of real interest to him as well as the management area best suited to his abilities. Such an opportunity is vitally important because the college graduate whose interests have crystallized and who has charted a definite course for his future is a rare individual.

"To achieve the higher echelons of management, one must be endowed with or develop self confidence. Large hotels provide this opportunity for the neophyte hotelman, as he is not immediately placed in a position of authority and responsibility. For some people the old sink or swim philosophy may be the correct prescription, but many potentially fine executives may be ruined by too sudden a dunking into the pool of executive responsibility. Such a situation most often occurs in the smaller hotel.

"The learning value of hotel experience correlates well with the training, experience and skill of the hotel personnel. Invariably the staff of a large hotel is the most experienced and possesses the widest range of abilities. While this experience cannot be assimilated by osmosis, the opportunity to work with this caliber personnel rates as one of the major advantages of large hotel training.

"Most college people seek, consciously or subconsciously, a position in which they can use initiative. Large hotel supervision and management offer the greatest challenge to one's initiative.

"There are various problems encountered in the large hotel. To meet and solve these problems will be considered an advantage by some people and a disadvantage by others. A description of large hotel experience would be incomplete without a statement of these problems. Very briefly they are:

"1. One must learn to administer larger groups of employees.
"2. Communications to and from the staff are complicated by the larger size of the organization.
"3. To make good, one must recognize the possibility of being lost in a large company.

"I would also ask that students consider the apparent disadvantages:

"1. The initial pay is lower *if* it is compared with a job of key responsibility in a smaller property. The choice between immediate financial reward with responsibility and a lower salary with training is not an easy one to make.

"2. The pace of activities is greater, thus there is more demand on personal energies in a large property.

"3. When one wishes to relax, sports and recreational facilities are not usually close by.

"4. Participation in community activities is not possible as soon, nor as completely, as in a smaller organization.

"Perhaps a brief summary would be to restate the case as follows:

"If one enjoys a sense of team participation, the satisfaction of group acceptance, and the challenge of achievements through the training and encouragement of groups of people, then I believe he will find it to be at its fullest development within a large hotel."

CHAPTER 8

A Look into the Future

Although change and obsolescence have always been an integral part of the hospitality industry, hotelmen have never before faced the tremendous acceleration of change that has taken place in every way of life during the past few years. Consequently, a look into the future becomes more of a business necessity and less of a pleasant pastime to while away a few hours. To predict the future, however, has become no easier than it was in the past. Since my crystal ball is rather cloudy, and I can lay no claim to visionary powers, my predictions can only come from close scrutiny of developing trends and from the thinking and educated guesses of my colleagues and myself.

A number of areas promising significant changes come to mind immediately. The eleven areas chosen for discussion are:

1. New Developments in Tourism
2. Changes in Transportation
3. The Role of Marketing
4. Future Developments of Motels and Motor Hotels
5. Science and the Problems of the Hotel Industry
6. The Small Community Hotel
7. Automation in Hotels
8. The Role of Research
9. Data Processing
10. The Food Service of the Future
11. The "Blue Sky" Future

NEW DEVELOPMENTS IN TOURISM

Today, tourism is both the fastest growing and the largest industry in the world. Because of this growth, a number of factors are coming into proper focus and we find that what have always been considered separate industries are now, in reality, integral parts of a much larger industry—tourism. Two very specific ones are the airlines and the hotels. While some relationship has always existed, the future will find hotels and airlines so closely correlated and coordinated that it will take more than a cursory glance to tell them apart.

Pan American Airways visualized this relationship years ago when the company organized Intercontinental Hotels as a wholly owned subsidiary. The growth of this hotel system almost exactly parallels the growth of tourism in the world. The past five years reveal tremendous acceleration. Further proof of the desirability of this relationship came recently when Trans World Airlines purchased Hilton International Company, which operated more than 40 hotels around the world. More mergers of this type are almost certain to take place in the very near future.

Perhaps even more important than the mergers will be a closer relationship between hotel and airlines, with each incorporating some aspects of the other. Reservations, tickets, check-in, and up-to-date information will be available right in the hotel. No longer will the guest check out, travel to the airport, and then discover his flight canceled. While the airport comes to the hotel, the hotel will also go to the airport. The moment the guest steps out of the plane, he will be in the capable hands of hotel personnel.

Soon the tourist will travel anywhere, fully serviced, yet receive only one bill when he gets home. In the hotel he will be kept up to date on flight information and told when he will be transported to the airport. He will pack his luggage, leave his room, enter the limousine for the airport, move into his assigned airline seat, and take off for his next destination. Upon landing he will be received by the hotel, whisked to the hotel itself, and ushered to his room, where he will find his luggage awaiting him. No waits, no lines, no delays, no cash to fumble with—all this should be with us in a very few years.

A new concept of management is evolving as a direct result of the growth of tourism. Traditionally, there have been some considerable differences between the American and the European approaches to the profession of hotel management. While each approach has its advocates, the question of which is better is no longer pertinent. The goal, today, is to create an international concept of hotel operation. This new concept will incorporate the best of the European and American modes of operation and continue to develop from that point. Within a few years, the international traveler will demand the level of service possible only under the new international concept of hotel operation.

When Conrad Hilton launched Hilton International and proclaimed his belief that such an operation would be an instrument to promote international understanding, many people scoffed at the idea as being idealistic or called it just another business promotion campaign. Today many of the same people willingly admit that Hilton's vision and foresight were indeed valid and praiseworthy. It is not difficult to visualize a Center of

Tourism and International Studies being built and operated within the next few years. I picture it closely associated with a major university which will provide the theorists from many academic disciplines to tackle the complex and challenging problems of a world grown small and intimate. The catalyst will be tourism; its components will be transportation and hospitality. Already tourism has contributed to international understanding. It is quite possible that tourism may produce results that diplomacy has never been able to achieve.

CHANGES IN TRANSPORTATION

The hotel world appears to have grasped the full significance of the relationship between mode of transportation and the character of hotel operation. However, hotelmen are only now adjusting fully to the impact of the "jet age," which has been with us for over a decade. There will be no opportunity to relax or to congratulate ourselves on how well we met the challenge. Already new challenges are just ahead and the planning must move into high gear now!

The so called Jumbo Jets are a reality and will soon be in operation commercially. They are certain to create some interesting problems and to precipitate changes in the hotel field. Capable of carrying over 400 passengers, a jumbo jet is bound to have an effect on terminal operations. Picture two jumbo jets arriving within minutes of each other at about the time two others are loading for departure. It is doubtful if a single terminal building in the country is capable of handling this mob of 1600 people under present mode of operation. But let the weather close in and cancel two or three departures. Suddenly the hotel lobby is jammed with delayed passengers, each one wanting his room back only to learn that most of the rooms are already booked. Obviously, hotels will face some new challenges.

Perhaps the most important effect of the jumbo jet will be to lower airline fares considerably. For the first time, the price of airline tickets will come within the budget range of millions of Americans and citizens of many other countries as well. When one considers that currently seven out of every ten United States citizens have never flown in an airplane, the size of this potential market is a staggering figure. The jumbo jets are scheduled for both national and international flights, so the increased travel will affect both national and international hotels. Ever increasing numbers of Americans will travel abroad, widening the tourism market.

The combination of lower airline fares and increased prosperity in many foreign countries will finally bring many foreign visitors to the Unted States. At present, the majority of American hotels is not completely equipped to service this market. Today most foreign visitors who patronize hotels speak English and thus create no communication problem. The new market will not be so versatile and the hotels will, of necessity, place emphasis on having a number of multilingual personnel on the staff. A modified version of the concierge may well become standard in United States hotels catering to international guests.

The jumbo jet will provide both positive and negative influences to the hotel industry in the United States. My projections indicate that the positive influences far outweigh the negative ones. It appears almost certain that the new plane will accelerate the development of airport motels and hotels.

Just when the hotelman really comes "to grips" with the challenges of the jumbo jet, the "supersonic jet age" will be upon him. This proposed plane with the ability to carry passengers from New York to London in two hours may well revolutionize the hotel industry. Based on current data, which is at best very sketchy, the author believes that the great changes will come with the jumbo jet. No great changes are foreseen for the hotel operator when the supersonics go into full operation.

THE ROLE OF MARKETING

Marketing relates directly to the customer and the service he receives or buys. A service industry, which hotel management is, would be expected to be marketing minded. To quote Professor Edward Bursk, "It is a paradox that most service industries are usually service-minded, always cost-minded—but seldom marketing-minded." The situation will change radically within the next few years for a variety of reasons.

For many years, hotels have been designed, constructed, and operated primarily by standards developed by hoteliers. Fortunately it worked out well. What the hotelmen had, the public enjoyed and patronized. Times are changing; people are changing. Because of these factors, the old market has all but disappeared. Future business must come from a new group of people and, like it or not, hotels must cater to the needs, desires, and tastes of this market if they want their business. In order to cater to these needs, the needs must first be identified. This is the role of marketing, which will play a prominent role in the hotel industry. Tomorrow's hotels and services will be based on what the guest wants and likes—not merely on what the hotelman thinks or decides the guest will want.

Anyone who is pessimistic about the future of the hospitality industry must have overlooked some huge potential markets nearly ripe for plucking. Already mentioned are the jumbo and supersonic jets which should increase the number of people traveling. Then one should review the latest data on discretionary income of Americans. From 1950-1966 the discretionary income in the United States grew 237 percent. From 1966-1971 it will increase an additional 41 percent and is projected to increase at least 5 percent per year after that. In brief, there are more people with more money with more leisure time.

To attract this market poses a few problems. The majority of the individuals are not current hotel customers nor do they very closely resemble today's hotel patron. In the first place, over half the population of the United States has never spent one single night in a motel or hotel—in fact, has never even been inside a hotel or motel. If we are to sell him on our hotel we need to know something about him. The information will come from marketing.

Next we come to what is affectionately called the "new breed." Many people realize the tremendous changes in age distribution occurring in the United States. By 1970, 50 percent of the population will be 25 years old or under. Combine this fact with data on marriage at an earlier age (about 18 for American girls) and the increasing senior citizen segment of the population, and you have spotlighted tomorrow's mass market. Both national and international hotels want data on this group because it appears so radically different in comparison to today's market. Hotels must look to marketing for the answers. In my opinion, *marketing* will be the hotelman's most valuable resource in the foreseeable future.

FUTURE DEVELOPMENT OF MOTELS AND MOTOR HOTELS

Many people consider motels a particularly American phenomenon and refuse to consider the international possibilities. The future of motels in the United States was well covered in the opening chapter. But what is the story beyond the boundaries of the United States of America? When motor car travel becomes heavy in any part of the world, the motels will soon begin to spring up. The two go hand in hand. The real boom period for motels in Europe should be the 1970's. Already the foundation is in place, and development is picking up speed. Major oil companies are providing the leadership and the money for European motel development. The familiar Esso trademark of Standard Oil of New Jersey now appears on 14 motels located in Sweden, Denmark, Germany, Italy, and England. The company projects 10 new motels yearly for several years and expansion into Norway, the Netherlands, Belgium and Austria. Besides Esso, one finds the Italian group AGRIP as a forerunner in European motel development. Rank Motor Inns, Holiday Inns, Travelodge, Howard Johnson, and Treadway are all interested and in various stages of exploration, construction, and operation. It won't be long before Europeans come to recognize the big green sign or the orange roof.

Most other parts of the world do not appear ready for motel development. Only when good highways are filled with autos carrying families and businessmen considerable distances will motels enter the picture. Eventually the rest of the world will enjoy motels, if they haven't first become obsolete.

SCIENCE AND THE PROBLEMS OF THE HOTEL INDUSTRY

If asked their opinion whether hotel management was an art or a science, many people would say art. A tendency to believe this opinion and also to believe that the hotel business was unique and thus could not utilize modern management practices created a serious situation for the industry. Fortunately in the 1960's scientists began to peruse the industry closely. They soon found that hotels make an excellent setting for research studies.

The food scientist was first into the field. Highly skilled culinary personnel are becoming very, very scarce. The prognosis was for an even greater scarcity in a few years. The food scientist is now working on frozen, dehydrated, freeze dry, irradiated, and canned food for use in the industry. The goal is to produce food of equal quality to fresh and at the same time to accomplish this with far fewer skilled culinarians.

Even greater than the skill problems are the human problems of management. Perhaps in no other field is there the continuous interaction among people found in hotels. The guest, of course, interacts with the employees. Psychologists and sociologists should find hotels some of the finest research grounds ever explored.

Hotels must rely heavily on marketing, advertising, and sales promotion. Each of these areas has psychological undertones. Among the employees one finds morale problems, training, productivity, recruitment, grievance, and communication problems. Every sign says these areas will get worse before they get better. Sociologists and psychologists are badly needed. In the next ten years both groups will be reporting studies on hotel groups and relating new management approaches to the hotel executives. It should be a happy marriage.

THE SMALL COMMUNITY HOTEL

The older hotel in the smaller cities and communities has been pretty well written off as a total loss by most people in the industry. Some of these properties appear to merit a better future than demolition. In practically every case, the rooms are no longer competitive and will be channeled to other uses. However, the community needs a central point where meetings, banquets, receptions, and the like can be held and properly serviced. Businessmen want a central location where luncheon is available, a cocktail lounge is operating, and dinner may be purchased. For years the hotel was the focal point and the status badge of the community. Sentimental reasons motivate attempts to keep these hotels operating. It appears that someone has missed a good bet in the food and beverage areas of these hotels.

In many cases, the market is present for food, beverage, and banquet business. The hotel is reasonably well equipped to handle the volume. What is needed is young, progressive management. Sooner or later, one or more smart young men will form a company designed to operate the food and beverage facilities of these hotels under management contracts or possibly a lease arrangement. The company will program a complete program from merchandising to menu planning and decoration to standardized procedures. Already we have contract food service management in industrial plants, hospitals, department stores, colleges, and schools. A logical extension of the same concept is into the community hotels. I predict that this development will become a reality within five years.

AUTOMATION

The latest manpower projections for the hospitality industry indicate a need for 250,000 new people every year for the foreseeable future; 185,000 of this total would be needed in positions which are semiskilled or below. To recruit this number of people will be an almost insurmountable challenge unless some rather dramatic and unfortunate economic changes occur. But even if the industry were to find them, it might not be able to afford them. If employee productivity were to continue at the current level and wages continue to spiral, we would be dealing primarily in red ink.

The challenge is to retain the personal service and hospitality of the business while automating everything possible. Certainly the trend is to more and more self service even in the so-called service industries; the telephone company is a good illustration. Whether hotels can go as far without alienating customers is a vital question. It now seems likely that they will explore all other possibilities before moving toward less personal service. Automation and mass production are coming to the back of the house operation and to all behind the scenes activity just as rapidly as equipment and techniques become available. The areas of food preparation, production and service, record keeping, laundry, and housekeeping will be analyzed and automated as rapidly and completely as possible. The design of new guest rooms and other public rooms will attempt to keep manpower requirements at a minimum. Many mechanical and electronic devices will replace human effort in these areas. While some of the services become depersonalized, the service is accomplished so much faster, better, and more accurately that the guest willingly accepts it as progress. The automation trend is established and should accelerate during the next few years.

THE ROLE OF RESEARCH

In the first edition of this book appeared the prediction, ". . . the hotel industry will sponsor a full fledged research program aimed at designing the efficient hotel of tomorrow." The full fledged program is not in existence, but the industry certainly has become very research conscious. The impetus came from the Statler Foundation, which gave a grant of $500,000 to Cornell University's School of Hotel Administration to inaugurate a research program for the hotel industry. Since its inception, the research division has found plenty of challenges and made some excellent contributions to the field. The Ready Food Concept and a Data Processing System are two of the best known contributions.

There is much to be learned about building and decorating materials, automated equipment, new products, and much more. The research will be both applied and pure, technical and theoretical. In one section basic testing of mattresses, wall covering, carpeting, and food recipes may be underway while right next door a "dreamer" is already approaching the "hotel and tourist climate" we can expect in the year 2000.

The relationship among universities and the industry will grow closer and closer. Research plays a major role in a university providing experience and feedback for the student, intellectual stimulation for the professor, and new frontiers for the industry. Although to date industry has provided more moral than financial support for research, the years to come will see a highly organized, well-financed research program fully supported by both industry and education.

DATA PROCESSING

Data Processing is a very simple function which is destined to play a major role in changing our whole way of life. Apparently the extent to which this function can be developed is nearly limitless, while there is no limit to the ways in which it can be used.

Data processing is based upon something or nothing. Either there is or there isn't a hole in a certain place on a card. There is either an electric impulse or no electric impulse. We do not need to elaborate upon the apparent miracles performed through the use of this simple concept. Contrary to many beliefs, there is no capacity to reason or to think incorporated in the equipment. Thinking and reasoning are unique to man. Data processing is the product of man's ability in these two areas. Man is still the master.

Data processing can be divided into two fields: scientific and commercial. The development, use, and success of data processing in the scientific world has been fantastic. In the commercial field, however, development has been simple, and use has been limited and marked by failure more often than by success. Perhaps as much as 95 percent of the commercial use of data processing is in the nature of more sophisticated bookkeeping machines, which still depend on manual operations similar to those required for adding machines. There is little reduction in cost from that of other existing bookkeeping machines. However, the final output is usually available sooner, in greater accuracy and with more detail from the same input.

Results in the commercial field lag far behind those in the scientific field. There is a paradox which may explain this limited development. Like micro-ovens in the kitchen, computers have a great deal of romance attached to them. A businessman often heard others speak knowingly of the miracles computers could perform. Having no experience with and little knowledge of these computers, the man felt a little inferior and out of place.

He was determined that his company would stay abreast of the times. If that meant having a computer, then, by golly, the company would buy one. Having purchased the equipment, the next step was to find a use for the new installation. The final result was often disappointing. Strangely enough, the very people who were so rash as to jump blindly into data processing are now the ones resisting available highly sophisticated uses.

Data processing is a simple concept. The equipment required to handle it, however, is extremely complex and very costly. The concept and the machine must be brought together by what is called programming. It is not essential here to describe the specifics of programming other than to state that it is a long, hard process requiring many man days, and the cost is high.

A significant characteristic of data processing is its extremely high speed of functioning, which makes possible an unbelievable capacity for work or output. Commerce has this fine tool available but just does not use it to gain the terrific potential available. Why? Perhaps the answer lies in the fact that scientists are accustomed to joint efforts while businessmen are inclined to go it alone. Data processing has a high cost which is matched by a high capacity to work, but only when the work is highly repetitive. Relatively speaking, there are few single enterprises which can afford a very sophisticated data processing system. Even if there were, there would not be enough repetitive work to keep it operating. Another reason for the discrepancy between scientific and commercial comes from the approach. Much that the scientist seeks from data processing would be impossible to obtain without it. The scientist must have data processing regardless of cost. The businessman must measure the cost and be reasonably assured that the installation will lead to greater profits.

In spite of the problems involved, there are in existence a few highly sophisticated systems, although they usually serve only one large enterprise. An example is the reservations system of American Airlines, which is said to have cost about $45 million. Even this system lacks some sophistication. It does not handle all the reservations. However, there is no information whether the cost of this system plus the cost of the manual handling portion is any less than a completely manual operation would be.

What does all this mean to the hotel industry? The ramifications for hotel operation are as great, or greater, than for any other industry. Hotels need considerable amounts of information for guidance in operations. Since the turn of the century there have been repeated efforts to establish a system to collect this data, but none have been completely successful. A sophisticated data processing is the answer to this situation. Unfortunately, both its cost and capacity are too high to be successful in any one hotel. In January 1966, the Research Section of Cornell's School of Hotel Administration outlined a sophisticated, practical system which required groups of hotels to join together in utilizing it. Hotels were hesitant to do so and little progress was made. The National Cash Register Company has contracted with the same Research Section for final designing of a complete system which the National Cash Register Company will make available for hotels. Many believe this is the breakthrough the industry has been awaiting.

Hotels have never been able to exploit their market. In fact, until the great depression hotels sat back and waited for the guest to walk in. Then Ralph Hitz opened the Hotel New Yorker in New York City. Mr. Hitz kept an up-to-date file on each of his guests. Legend has it that in one year Hitz hired 50 assistant managers with their guest lists from other hotels. Statler gave each guest a copy of the local paper. Hitz gave the guest a copy of his hometown newspaper. Other hotels soon copied the guest history idea and it became standard procedure for most hotels. It is also true that to maintain and analyze a guest history file becomes a very costly practice. Consequently, most hotels have been forced to give up the guest history file primarily for economic reasons. A hotel utilizing sophisticated data processing would have all the potential of a comprehensive guest history system at no actual cost. The file would be kept up to the minute and accurate as a by-product of other operations.

Now let's look at other applications to hotel operation. If the creation of a restaurant check is designed to record automatically all the data in the system, then there will be a 100 percent agreement between the data in the system and that on the check. True, a waiter might serve a steak and put chicken on the check, but other controls will catch it. Anyway, the check says the waiter served chicken and the data in the system shows he served chicken. Furthermore, the chicken is recorded in the system and must be accounted for. The record is even there to explain why a steak is unaccounted for and a chicken is left over. It is available to help determine whether the error was by design or accidental.

Here is another example. Food in the storeroom is recorded in the system. Issues are recorded semi-automatically. The system now automatically tells the purchasing agent when to replenish the stock. It gives him the standards that apply to the product, the normal quantity to buy and the full record of the last three purchases. If any objection to the product has been recorded by the chef, this information will also be reported. If desired, the system can automatically give an order to the supplier.

When the new goods are received, a new entry is made in the system. If the old standards still hold, they are recorded automatically. If the price has changed, this is recorded too. The old stock will be issued at the old price and the new stock at the new price automatically.

The new input will be checked automatically against the purchase order for verification. A notice will be given to the supplier that the specific goods have been accepted at the stated price and the company acknowledges an account payable on that basis. Any applicable discounts will be made. On the proper day a check in favor of the supplier automatically will be drawn for the proper amount, executed, and mailed to the supplier. The supplier's account in Accounts Payable, the bank balance, and all other related accounts will be posted. But such accomplishments are only a beginning.

Hotels have, at best, rather dull tools to control expenses, especially expenses in food operations. Each day a figure (probably 100 percent estimate) has been used to record food cost. This is not cost of an individual item but the total cost of all food sold in the hotel that day. At least the revenue figure should be accurate. But about the only control, until a new inventory has been taken, is the percentage of the estimated cost to the total revenue. For years attempts have been made to operate a quantity control. In such a system, the quantity of food consumed or missing is calculated against the number of portions sold. Some systems tried to control 100 or more items while others reduced this number to about 20 key items representing the majority of the dollar volume. Sooner or later, however, the outcome was the same. The controls were so far behind, so inaccurate, and so costly that they had to be dropped. Data processing can supply all of this data daily, accurately, and inexpensively, because it is a product of other operations.

It must be emphasized that these accomplishments all await one prerequisite. Hotel operators must join together to use a computer center. Only when the costs can be spread over thousands of rooms does the system become economical. The desire for privacy and secrecy appears to be holding back the hotel operators. Perhaps these fears are unfounded. A properly designed integrated system will assist in maintaining privacy. The input to the system is in little bits and pieces which have little relationship to the whole. The output can be restricted to one printer located in the general manager's office. While the computers in the center must be monitored periodically, the data monitored need not be significantly complete to be meaningful. Besides, the center will be manned by a small number of superior people possessing high moral and ethical standards. In comparison, hotel accounting today is done in an office where up to 100 people have access to private information. Employee turnover is reasonably high, which helps to magnify the problem.

In summary, a fully integrated, sophisticated data processing system will perform automatically all accounting and control functions from input by which data is entered only once and then, more often than not, automatically as a by-product of the transaction. Annual statements, income tax returns (employees as well as company), the issue of checks, accounts receivable statements, and many, many other items can be fully automatic.

Even if hotel operators continue to resist the center concept, sooner or later the economics of the hotel industry will force the development and use of a data processing system.

Hotel chains are growing rapidly by ownership, leasing, and franchising. In the future, the control and supervision of these chains will be from a central point where a computer not only records the affairs of the individual units but also, to a very great extent, directs the operations. All of the accounting will be automatic at the computer center.

From Cornell's Research Section comes an outline for a system of data processing to be used with a program of Ready Foods that is designed to direct and control a chain of restaurants, hotels, motels, or a combination of all. The system even controls the ingredients, both as to quantity and quality, used in every food recipe. Recipes, portion sizes, and prices can be set to meet the appetites, tastes, and needs of the various local markets where units are located. Once these systems become operative in hotels (and hopefully hotels will lead the way), they can be adapted to hospitals, department stores, and other operations.

Data processing has always been closely associated with credit card systems. Some interesting experiments have been tried and they tend to foretell the future. A bank on Long Island installed data processing, issued credit cards to residents, and arranged for acceptance by the merchants. A very high percentage of transactions in the town went through the system. Many industries simply transferred funds from the company account to the employees' account instead of issuing checks.

A vice president of the Bank of America visualized a central credit system based upon data processing, in which transfer of credits would replace cash payments and even accounts receivable. Carte Blanche was the first of the three largest credit card systems to adopt data processing. American Express and Diners Club soon followed.

These developments will lead to a lessening of cash transactions as well as a marked decrease in accounts receivable. There will be clearing houses (probably banks). Purchases will be chits, which will pass through the system like checks. The owner of each account will receive practically all his receipts by having chits credited to his account and, in turn, his expenses will be charged to his account. Instead of owing money by accounts payable here and there, he will have a line of credit with the bank. Cash and bank checks will not disappear, but they will become ever less important. A byproduct of this development will be a careful watch over one's credit rating.

Totally integrated data processing must come. The wise entrepreneur will not only prepare for it, but start immediately to exploit it. If Ralph Hitz were operating hotels today, he would already have such a system.

THE FOOD SERVICE OF THE FUTURE

A number of pressures are exerting a strong influence toward a changing concept of food production practices in the retail food service industry. Among them are the following.

1. As our economy expands and government continues to move in the direction of the welfare state concept, labor costs will continue to increase. The increase will be noted especially when labor cost is measured against units produced.

2. The overall quality of labor is being weakened because

of supply and demand inequities. As the supply of competent culinary employees dwindles, the quality of the products produced may well suffer. The present emphasis on technological training of potential culinary employees, rapidly expanding as it is, will not produce the numbers of skilled personnel necessary to meet the expanding needs of the industry.

3.　The increased mobility of the American traveler both by air and the new interstate highway systems makes it increasingly difficult to forecast accurately the sale of particular entrees in a specific food service unit.

4.　Consumer standards for determining "quality food" cover a broad spectrum. At one extreme we find the bona fide gourmet and his relative, the person who has traveled a little internationally and considers himself a gourmet or at least a connoisseur of fine food. At the opposite extreme the man who eats because food is necessary to maintain life, but whose taste would never be classified as discriminating. Even the early TV dinners satisfied this type of consumer. In between are many degrees of taste and preference. To further confuse the issue, any one individual may move from one group to another depending upon his mood and needs.

5.　Chain-operated middle-priced restaurants offering a fine variety of acceptable food will increase radically.

6.　The upgraded quality of convenience food produced by commercial food manufacturers is already forcing a critical review of traditional food preparation practices in many retail food service units.

7.　The increasingly narrow profit margin in the volume feeding area has produced a situation in which the individual operator finds it increasingly difficult to compete. For hotels, the specialty restaurant has been a profitable alternate.

To meet these pressures, two general systems are evolving, both of which feature the utilization of frozen entrees. One conclusion already appears valid: it is not practical at present to go into frozen entrees on a partial basis. The production of systemed quality at an acceptable economic level under the partial system is unsatisfactory due to staffing, equipment requirements, and production practices which will of necessity be duplicated. The experience of the Dutch Pantry, Marriott-Hot Shoppes, and Stouffer organizations supports this conclusion.

The two systems evolving with the use of new foods are the open system and the closed system. Under the open system, the individual food operator or the chain of units procures frozen items from commercial sources, stores them, reconstitutes, and merchandises them. This concept is a radical change from traditional restaurant operation. Under this system, the operator is, in some cases, limited to the quality and variety of foods maintained by the local food distributor or vendor.

Under the closed system, the individual operator or the chain manufactures, stores, reconstitutes, and merchandises the menu items from raw material to the customer's plate. Many large chain operators have been forced into the closed system to insure the quality of food offered to their customers. The Ready Foods program under development at the Cornell School of Hotel Administration is a closed system. It offers the individual operator an opportunity to use modern food methods in presenting varied menu items of a quality and at a cost which will meet the competition offered by the chains.

Commercial food manufactuers have made great strides in upgrading and improving the quality of their entree items. Variety is almost limitless. The quality of the products will be determined by the price the restaurant operator is willing to pay. The improvements in techniques or preparation and freezing have led to products which should permit the individual operator to compete both in quality and price with chains using the closed system.

Both systems offer maximum utilization of limited numbers of professionally trained culinarians. Under the Ready Foods program, for example, no longer will the kitchen produce a series of items for a given meal. A production run is accomplished to cover the requirements for periods up to 90 days. The items are inventoried until needed. One chef controls the efforts of all his subordinates in an unharried manufacturing process. Quality and quantity controls may be employed during any step of preparation, inventory storage, and the reconstitution process.

At present the freezing and holding equipment most economical and most easily controlled is mechanical. This type of equipment appears to be most suitable for use by the individual operator. The commercial producers and the chain organizations are moving toward the nitrogen freezing process. Future developments and refinements should bring nitrogen units within the economic capability of the individual operator before too long.

One of the major problems under either system is the current lack of a reconstituting apparatus for defrosting and reheating the entrees from the frozen state. Convection and conduction ovens, 15 p.s.i. steamers, microwave units, atmospheric steam heaters, water baths, and pulse infrared heaters are available. All of these have desirable features and limitations. Eventually a unit which will defrost and reheat an entree whether it is packaged in metal, glass, ceramic material, or polyester film will be developed. Until such equipment is available, the operator must select one packaging material and key the correct reconstitution apparatus to it.

It has often been stated, "Freshly cooked steak or roast beef will never be supplemented by the frozen variety." Techniques do exist for preparing and reconstituting these items. The market will be developed. Price and inventory advantages will force this evolution. Methods of presentation will be developed for these convenience items to make them comparable to the current items prepared by conventional methods.

Decor and merchandising features aimed at atmosphere and promotion of high quality foods are a major factor in the success of any food operation. With the new food production practices, atmosphere and merchandising will be even more vital to the restaurant's success. Presentation of a reconstituted Coq au Vin or a Beef Wellington will require the same professional flair as now.

The contention here being advanced may be summarized thus: American genius for mass production of finished goods is finally being applied to foods relating to retail food service units. We are in the midst of that revolution. The pace can only quicken as pressures increase and technology improves. One fact remains clear. Reversion to the old ways is not in the cards. There is no historical evidence of such reversion for any item once it has been developed and adapted satisfactorily to mass production methods.

Let us hope there will always be fine restaurants preparing foods in the classical manner as we know them, but be assured they will be rare.

THE "BLUE SKY" FUTURE

All previous predictions have been pretty well founded on developing trends. Most of them should happen. Now let us move way into the future, about the year 2015. Scientists even now are describing what life will be like in that period. Computerized robots will perform many functions now handled by man. These robots will prepare food, wash the dishes, do much of the cleaning around the hotel, weed and care for the gardens, and perform several types of office work.

Some rather significant transportation developments will have occurred. Trains traveling at speeds of 1,000 miles per hour will be commonplace. Underground and automated highways will handle, with great safety, a tremendous column of vehicular traffic. By air, a traveler will reach any point on earth in about two hours. There will be regular trips to the moon.

With regular travel to the moon there has to be a lunar hotel. Four students at Cornell's Hotel School decided not to wait until 2015, but went to work in 1967 to perform a feasibility study for a lunar hotel. Most people were amazed by the amount of information and facts these youngsters were able to compile. The report was serious in nature and ran to about 56 pages. Mr. Barron Hilton, President of Hilton Hotels Corporation, used the report as a basis for a talk he gave to the American Astronautical Society on lunar tourism. While not economically feasible, solutions for radiation, food, construction, and operational problems are included in this student report.

These same students came up with some other interesting information as a by-product of the lunar study. It seems that all the technical know-how and equipment exists today to build and operate a fine hotel under the sea. Equally as exciting is the possibility of building a completely temperature-conditioned resort and grounds almost anywhere in the world. Picture a semi-tropical resort placed in the middle of London or New York. The temperature would vary a maximum of two degrees. No fog, no smog, just pure fresh air, comfort conditioned. Remember: all this is possible right now. By the year 2015 these two developments will probably be old hat. Space travel, however, should still be unusual enough to serve as a status badge.

Undoubtedly the future holds many unforeseen challenges. No matter what they may be, it seems absolutely certain that the hotel industry will be there to meet them.

Appendix

FOUR-YEAR COLLEGES AND UNIVERSITIES
OFFERING MAJORS IN HOTEL ADMINISTRATION

Cornell University
School of Hotel Administration
Ithaca, New York

Florida State University
Department of Hotel and
    Restaurant Management
Tallahassee, Florida

Michigan State University
School of Hotel, Restaurant and
    Institutional Management
East Lansing, Michigan

Nevada Southern University
Department of Hotel Management
Las Vegas, Nevada

Oklahoma State University
Stillwater, Oklahoma

Pennsylvania State University
Department of Hotel Management
University Park, Pennsylvania

University of Denver
Department of Hotel Management
Denver, Colorado

University of Hawaii
Hotel, Restaurant and
    Tourism Administration
Honolulu, Hawaii

University of Massachusetts
Department of Hotel and
    Food Administration
Amherst, Massachusetts

University of New Hampshire
Department of Hotel Administration
Durham, New Hampshire

Washington State College
Department of Hotel Administration
Pullman, Washington

SOME JUNIOR COLLEGES AND TECHNICAL SCHOOLS OFFERING TRAINING FOR THE HOTEL INDUSTRY

Tuskegee Institute, Tuskegee, Alabama

Capuchino High School, San Bruno, California
Compton High School, Compton, California
John F. Kennedy High School, Richmond, California
Los Angeles Trade-Technical College, Los Angeles, California
Moorpark College, Moorpark, California
Pacific High School, San Leandro, California
San Bernardino Valley College, San Bernardino, California
City College of San Francisco, San Francisco, California
Sequoia High School, Redwood City, California
Tamalpais High School, Mill Valley, California
Emily Griffith Opportunity School, Denver, Colorado
Metropolitan State College, Denver, Colorado
Culinary Institute of America, Inc., New Haven, Connecticut
Manchester Community College, Manchester, Connecticut

Kent County Vocational-Technical Center, Woodside, Delaware

Junior College of Broward County, Fort Lauderdale, Florida
Lindsey Hopkins Education Center, Miami, Florida
Miami-Dade Junior College, Miami, Florida
Palm Beach Junior College, Lake Worth, Florida

Carver Vocational High School, Atlanta, Georgia

Washburne Trade School, Chicago, Illinois
Maine Township High School District #207, Park Ridge, Illinois

Delgado Trades & Technical Institute, New Orleans, Louisiana
Jefferson Parish Vocational-Technical School, Metairie, Louisiana

Southern Maine Vocational-Technical Institute, South Portland, Maine
Chef's Training Institute of New England, Boston, Massachusetts
Endicott Junior College, Beverly, Massachusetts

David Hale Fanning Trade High School, Worchester, Massachusetts
Food Research Center for Catholic Institutions,
    North Easton, Massachusetts
Chadsey High School, Detroit, Michigan
Lansing Community College, Lansing, Michigan
Oakland Community College, Union Lake, Michigan
Romulus Senior High School, Romulus, Michigan
Minneapolis Area Vocational-Technical School, Rochester, Minnesota
St. Paul Area Technical-Vocational Institute, St. Paul, Minnesota
Metropolitan Junior College, Kansas City, Missouri
St. Louis Jr. College District, St. Louis, Missouri

Central Nebraska Vocational-Technical School, Hastings, Nebraska
Thompson School of Applied Science, Durham, New Hampshire
Bergen County Vocational & Technical High School,
    Hackensack, New Jersey
Trenton Central High School, Trenton, New Jersey
Educational Institute of the American Hotel & Motel Assn.
    New York, New York
Chemung-Tioga Vocational-Technical High School,
    Horseheads, New York
Emerson Vocational High School, Buffalo, New York
Erie County Technical Institute, Buffalo, New York
Food and Maritime Trades High School, New York, New York
Ithaca-Tompkins-Seneca Vocational School, Ithaca, New York
New York City Community College, Brooklyn, New York
Paul Smith's College, Paul Smith, New York
Pratt Institute, Brooklyn, New York
Rochester Institute of Technology, Rochester, New York
State University Agricultural & Technical College,
    Alfred at Wellsville, New York
State University Agricultural and Technical College, Canton, New York
State University Agricultural and Technical College,
    Cobleskill, New York

State University Agricultural and Technical College, Delhi, New York
State University Agricultural and Technical College,
    Morrisville, New York
Sullivan County Community College, South Fallsburg, New York
Ashevill-Buncombe Technical Institute, Ashville, North Carolina
Durham Senior High School, Durham, North Carolina

Jane Addams Vocational High School, Cleveland, Ohio
Courter Technical High School, Cincinnati, Ohio
Cuyahoga Community College, Cleveland, Ohio
Norwood Technical School, Norwood, Ohio
Oklahoma State University, Okmulgee, Oklahoma
Portland Community College, Portland, Oregon
Lane Community College, Eugene, Oregon

Marrell Dobbins Technical High School, Philadelphia, Pennsylvania
Milton Hershey School, Hershey, Pennsylvania
Eastern Montgomery County Vocational-Technical School,
    Willow Grove, Pennsylvania
Hotel School of Puerto Rico, Sarranquitas, Puerto Rico
Inter American University, Hata Rey, Puerto Rico

University of Houston, Downtown School, Houston, Texas
Booker T. Washington High School, Houston, Texas

College of the Virgin Islands, St. Thomas, Virgin Islands

Eau Claire Vocational, Technical & Adult School,
    Eau Claire, Wisconsin
Madison Vocational & Adult School, Madison, Wisconsin
Milwaukee Institute of Technology, Milwaukee, Wisconsin

Canada
Cambrian College of Applied Arts & Technology,
    Sault Ste. Marie, Ontario

RECOMMENDED READINGS

Abbott, Karl P.
Open for the Season. Garden City, Doubleday, 1950. 278 pp.
Abraben, E.
Resort Hotels, Planning and Management. New York, Reinhold, 1965. 295 pp.
American Hotel Institute
Front Office Procedure. East Lansing, American Hotel Institute, Michigan State University, Kellogg Center, 1958.
Baum, Vicki
Grand Hotel (translated by Basil Creighton). Garden City, Doubleday, 1931. 309 pp.
Bolton, Whitney
The Silver Spade: The Conrad Hilton Story. New York, Farrar, Strauss and Young, 1954. 230 pp.
Brigham, Grace
Housekeeping for Hotels, Motels, Hospitals, Clubs, Schools. (revised.). New York, Ahrens, 1962. 158 pp.
Brodner, Joseph, Howard M. Carlson, and Henry T. Maschal (Eds.)
Profitable Food and Beverage Operation. New York, Ahrens, 1962. 458 pp.
Case, Frank
Tales of a Wayward Inn. New York, Garden City Publishing Company, 1940. 390 pp. (Out of print.)
Coffman, Charles Dewitt
The Full House. A Hotel/Motel Promotion Primer. Ithaca, Cornell University, School of Hotel Administration, 1964. 246 pp.
Dabney, Thomas Ewing
The Man Who Bought the Waldorf: The Life of Conrad Hilton. New York, Duell, Sloan and Pearce, 1950. 272 pp.
Doswell, Roger, and Philip
Case Studies in Hotel Management. London, Barrie & Rockliff, 1967. 138 pp.

Dukas, Peter
   Hotel Front Office Management in Operation. Dubuque, Wm. C. Brown, 1957. 150 pp.
Gunn, Claire A., and Robert McIntosh
   Motel Planning and Business Management. Dubuque, Wm. C. Brown, 1964. 233 pp.
Hilton, Conrad Nicholson
   Be My Guest. Englewood Cliffs, N.J., Prentice-Hall, 1957. 372 pp.
Horwath, Ernest B., Louis Toth, and John D. Lesure
   Hotel Accounting. New York, Ronald Press, 1963. 513 pp.
Jarman, Rufus
   A Bed for the Night: The Story of the Wheeling Bellboy, E. M. Statler, and His Remarkable Hotels. New York, Harper, 1952. 309 pp.
Lattin, Gerald W.
   Careers in Hotels and Restaurants. New York, Henry Z. Walck, 1967. 108 pp.
Lundberg, Donald
   Inside Innkeeping. Dubuque, Wm. C. Brown, 1956. 170 pp.
Lundberg, Donald, and James P. Armatas
   The Management of People in Hotels, Restaurants and Clubs. Dubuque, Wm. C. Brown, 1964. 231 pp.
Podd, George O., and John D. Lesure
   Planning and Operating Motels and Motor Hotels. New York, Ahrens, 1964. 343 pp.
Sonnabend, Roger P.
   Your Future in Hotel Management. New York, Richards Rosen, 1964. 158 pp.
Witzky, Herbert K.
   Modern Hotel-Motel Management Methods. New York, Ahrens, 1964. 278 pp.
Zwarensteyn, Hendrik
   Legal Aspects of Hotel Administration. East Lansing, Bureau of Business and Economic Research, Graduate School of Business Administration, Michigan State University, 1962. 456 pp.

Index